Closing the Gap Between Technology and Application

About the Book and Editor

Closing the Gap Between Technology and Application
James C. Emery, Series Editor

This comprehensive study of five major areas of computer application in higher education presents the viewpoints of both purveyors and users of computer technology. The material is based on the EDUCOM 1977 Fall Conference.

In the initial chapters of the book, Peter Roll and C. A. Conover offer a general perspective on the use of computing in higher education, noting that the use of small machines in a distributed fashion is changing the organization and application of computers on campus today. In succeeding chapters, the highlighted areas—office automation, distributed academic computing, distributed administrative computing, instructional systems, and information resources—are each examined with a three-part approach. First, technical issues related to the specific area are presented, then administrative issues are explored, and finally a reaction and overview are provided. The contributors recognize the gap that exists between the potential of computer technology for higher education and the reality of current applications; they all identify specific problems in their areas and suggest approaches to solving those problems.

The concluding chapter addresses the technology transfer process in colleges and universities. Donald Smith advances the theory that the compatability of new technologies in distributed computing with the traditional distributed nature of higher education may well contribute to the rapid and effective use of computers in higher education.

James C. Emery has been president of EDUCOM since 1976. He previously served as director of computing activities at the University of Pennsylvania and as chairman of the Decision Sciences Department of the Wharton School of Business.

Closing the Gap Between Technology and Application

Proceedings of the 1977 EDUCOM Fall Conference

James C. Emery, Series Editor

Routledge
Taylor & Francis Group
LONDON AND NEW YORK

First published 1978 by Westview Press

Published 2018 by Routledge
52 Vanderbilt Avenue, New York, NY 10017
2 Park Square, Milton Park, Abingdon, Oxon OX14 4RN

Routledge is an imprint of the Taylor & Francis Group, an informa business

Library of Congress Cataloging in Publication Data
Main entry under title:
Closing the gap between technology and application.
(EDUCOM series in computing and telecommunication in higher education; v. 1)
1. Education—Data processing—Addresses, essays, lectures. 2. Computer-assisted instruction—Addresses, essays, lectures. I. Emery, James C. II. Educom. III. Series: Educom. Educom series in computing and telecommunication in higher education; v. 1.
LB2846.C563 378'.0028'5 78-2233

ISBN 13: 978-0-367-01757-6 (hbk)
ISBN 13: 978-0-367-16744-8 (pbk)

Contents

Preface

With this volume of proceedings, EDUCOM initiates a series in computing and telecommunication in higher education to be published by Westview Press. The series will include EDUCOM conference proceedings and monographs that result from research projects. Through the Westview series, we hope to share the results of common experience and research directed at problems of immediate importance to colleges and universities. By publishing with a major academic publisher, we can make our proceedings and research reports widely available.

Closing the Gap Between Technology and Application provides readers with analyses, from three points of view, of the use of computing technology in higher education. Several areas of application are considered from the point of view of the computer technician (technical issues), the administrator (administrative issues), and the user (reaction and overview). Application areas considered are office automation, distributed academic computing, distributed administrative computing, instructional systems, and information resources. To set the issue papers in perspective, this volume opens with general commentary from Peter Roll and C. A. Conover and closes with a paper by Donald Smith on technology transfer in the university.

Revised and edited for publication, these papers were originally presented at the EDUCOM Fall Conference in Minneapolis, Minnesota, October 26-28, 1977. Peter Roll served as conference chairman. Both the conference and this proceedings provide an opportunity for college faculty and administrators to share current ideas and experience with the application of computing in colleges and universities. I believe that readers will find this volume useful and informative.

James C. Emery
President, EDUCOM

1

Distributed Computing on Campus: An Introduction

Peter Roll

It was about twenty years ago that computers began to be used in significant ways in the academic programs and some of the business operations of colleges and universities. During the past two decades we have learned some things about effective and ineffective ways to manage, plan, and budget for computing services in higher education. EDUCOM, since its founding thirteen years ago, has helped in this learning process, especially through its role in bringing computer center and technical experts together with college and university administrators. Recently, EDUCOM has concentrated on network sharing of computer-based resources. Several conferences have been devoted to this subject and EDUNET is now a reality, even though it is not yet exactly a household word.

When program planning for EDUCOM's 1977 Fall Conference began in 1976, it was decided that the time was ripe to discuss distributed computing services and some of the applications that were becoming possible and economically feasible as a result of combining the entire spectrum of computing facilities—from microcomputers and minicomputers through large computer centers—with a network. Five application areas were selected: Office Automation, Distributed Academic Computing, Distributed Administrative Computing, Instructional

Systems, and Information Resources. It was also decided to place more emphasis on smaller facilities and to slant the program toward persons with administrative responsibilities for planning, budgeting, managing, and determining policy for computing services in colleges and universities. For this reason, each session was planned to include an overview or tutorial on the capabilities of the technology, plus a discussion of the planning, budgeting, management, and policy issues that concern college and university administrators.

This outline of the program had initially been completed eight or nine months before the conference. To the surprise of some of us and the expectation of others, there was a major economic breakthrough in the cost of microcomputer systems during the months between that time and the conference. Microcomputer technology has been with us for a few years, but in the last few months, the costs of complete and rather impressive systems have dropped by a factor of two or more to the point where some applications have for the first time become feasible or truly competitive with services from large computers. The September issue of *Scientific American* is devoted to microelectronics and provides clear evidence of this development. The articles are impressive, but the advertisements for microsystems are even more impressive. With Heathkit and Radio Shack entering the field, the economics of mass production for a consumer market are going to bring capabilities to higher education that technology alone could never achieve. We are standing on the threshold of a new generation of computing applications that will be at least as significant to higher education—and at least as much of a change—as were the operating systems of the so-called second generation and the time sharing, remote access, and multiprogramming that came with the third generation of computers. In this respect, the timing of the 1977 Fall Conference program could not have been more fortunate.

Along with opportunities for important new applications, there are some real management challenges and dangers. Managers of university computing services are going to have to devise new ways to plan, budget, and manage decentralized and distributed systems and the information they contain. Even though the hardware and the information may be decentralized, there will be the same or even greater needs as exist in centralized computing centers for system and applications software development, maintenance, compatibility, standards, common data element definitions, documentation, and sharing. In order to manage these kinds of problems, colleges and universities will need the technical and management expertise and leadership of their computer centers; the staffs of these centers will have to change and adapt their perspectives and skills very rapidly to new ways of delivering services (in some cases new and different services). More and more, we will need within large institutions and among groups of institutions of all sizes the kind of user services and facilitating networks that were recommended by the 1972-1973 Arlie House Conferences on National Computer Networking sponsored by EDUCOM and the National Science Foundation.

The 1977 EDUCOM Fall Conference was not expected to develop solutions to these kinds of problems; it was the expectation of the conference committee that some of the important issues would be identified and that this would start many of us thinking seriously about the administrative problems. As I believe the papers in this proceedings volume demonstrate, this expectation has been realized. Just as there have been several EDUCOM conferences on national networking over the past five or six years, I am sure this will be one of a series of conference programs devoted to the problems of effectively developing and using applications of distributed computing and information systems, integrating microelectronic technology into such systems, and integrating the systems in turn into larger networks, including ones of national scope. In two or three years, another conference may well focus again on many of these problems, but with the advantage of considerably more experience and consequently a somewhat clearer vision of the future than most of us have now.

Conference Issues

With this perspective, the thirteenth annual EDUCOM Fall Conference opened on the afternoon of Wednesday, October 26, 1977, at the Radisson Hotel in Minneapolis, Minnesota. The program began with a keynote address, "Closing the Gap Between Technology and Application," in which C. Allen Conover, vice president for systems planning and programs of Honeywell Information Systems, provided a review of the electronic and systems technology on which the current generation of computer technology is based, why and how this technology developed, and the applications problems it creates. Two days later, Donald K. Smith, senior vice president of the University of Wisconsin system, closed the conference with thoughtful comments on the technology transfer process in colleges and universities, the relationships among computing organizations, and the environment of colleges and universities today.

Plenary sessions provided an overview of the technology and the administrative issues in each of the five specific application areas named earlier. The speakers at these sessions identified a number of specific technical and administrative issues and generated some vigorous discussion. A number of issues kept recurring throughout the presentations and the discussions that concluded each session. On some of these issues there seemed to be a general consensus among the speakers and participants, while on others, points of disagreement were clearly represented.

Points of General Consensus

1. The foreseeable future for applications of technology in higher education will be characterized, above all, by rapid change, to which institutions will have to respond.

2. Distributed systems and microcomputers will characterize computing services in colleges and universities in the foreseeable future.

3. Although hardware development is progressing rapidly,

good software packages for applications and for the control of the processes of distributed computing are not yet available.

4. As hardware costs decline, the personnel costs associated with computing services will continue to be an important consideration, making it feasible (and in some cases desirable) to acquire excess hardware that is underutilized if it will improve the productivity of staff.

5. The fiscal and demographic outlook for higher education in the foreseeable future suggests that computing and other technologies and supporting services (including library services) will probably have to survive, change, and grow without consuming an increasing fraction of college and university budgets.

6. Because of the great fiscal pressures on institutions, decisions on the acquisition and use of computer and other technologies will favor the alternative with the lowest cost to the unit making the decision. Careful attention to the decision and funding process will be required to ensure that such decisions in fact entail the lowest cost to, and are in the best long-range interests of, the entire institution.

7. In order to support the growth of cost-effective applications of computer technology in the near future, high priority will have to be given to the establishment of appropriate support services and technical standards for the distributed facilities and services. In addition, experimentation and the sharing of knowledge, experience, and products resulting from it should be encouraged.

8. School and college administrators and policymakers in higher education will have to acquire a high degree of computer management literacy to cope effectively with the technical environment of the future.

Points of Disagreement

1. The Carnegie Commission report *The Fourth Revolution: Instructional Technology in Higher Education* (1972) predicted that computer and communications technologies would penetrate higher education to an important extent during the decade

1990-2000. Differing opinions were expressed at the conference as to whether the pace of technological change would bring penetration earlier than 1990, or whether the major impediments to technology in higher education (fiscal constraints and innate conservatism) would delay it into the next century.

2. A related question is whether we are facing a revolution in higher education brought about by the rapid rate of technological change, or an evolutionary development.

3. Differing views were expressed on whether higher education will have to change and adapt its organizational structures to utilize computer and communications technology effectively or whether the technology can be adapted to higher education. Donald K. Smith, in his closing address, offers the observation that the shift from centralized computer centers to distributed processing and microcomputers may well represent a natural development of technology in a direction that is much more suited to, and consistent with, the highly decentralized and conservative nature of higher education in the United States and Canada.

4. Related to the above issue is the question of whether financing and control should be distributed along with the components of the computing system: is the czar or the coordinator model most suited to higher education in the future?

The points on which a general consensus emerged represent some of the important characteristics of the technology and the technological change that we face, and of the environment in which applications must function. Each institution must recognize these characteristics and devise its own ways of managing them.

Conclusion

The conference did not develop any solutions to the problems associated with applications of distributed processing and microcomputers in higher education. However, there was general agreement that this is the trend of the future, and a number of the important issues were identified and discussed. This was the first EDUCOM conference devoted directly to applications of this technology. Several conferences have been devoted to networking over a period of years. One of the main agenda items for the future will be how to integrate mini- and micro-level technology into networks and into EDUNET in particular. Sharing and facilitating mechanisms will be as important for distributed and micro technology as they are for larger centralized computer centers. In two or three years, it may be appropriate for another EDUCOM conference to focus again on some of these problems with the advantage of more experience with applications of the technology.

2

Closing the Gap Between Technology and Application

C. A. Conover

Technology and Development Directions

This paper explores technology development beginning with the current usage of large systems today and the major influencing factors affecting that usage. It examines technology and system trends, and includes projections for future large systems revealing the emerging influence of minis. After showing the evolution of distributed processing, I will attempt to close the gap by reviewing user requirements on the processing network and the impact of these requirements on the vendor, the user, and the academic world.

The Data Processing World Today

Like the business environment, the data processing world is changing. While the user community is still heavily committed to batch applications, more and more companies are implementing transaction-oriented and online data base solutions. Most big users now employ large central systems with significant amounts of remote job entry and time sharing; yet these firms are facing growing demands from their end-user organizations to provide local processing power through minicomputers or intelligent terminals. One might call it a mini-revolution. Rising labor costs and rising demand are being offset by dramatic improvements in equipment price and performance. End-user organizations, with an eye on those labor costs, want to achieve direct access to computers, but without incurring the overhead of local conventional programming groups. Therefore, they want systems that are easier for nonspecialists to use. There are also pressures resulting from privacy legislation and data security requirements. Decentralization of computing power increases the risk of computer abuse and, therefore, the importance of preventing it.

In summary, there is considerable pressure bearing on the data processing industry to bring about change in the way data is processed. In fact, technology is advancing at a pace to respond to this pressure.

Technology and Systems Trends

Most people consider technology to be hardware technology, that is, circuits. While circuits are important, they tend to be only a part of technology. Additionally, technology is how to put those circuits together or interconnect them, and how to do it in an economical manner. For example, even though electricity moves at the speed of light, or about one foot in one one-billionth of a second, computer developers optimize to get circuits as close together as possible to cut down on delay times.

Beyond hardware technology is the even more important ingredient, systems technology. Software is the most important part of systems technology, and the driving force behind much development today. Systems technology is taking all the boxes—call them computers, communications modems, terminals—and linking them together in a manner that permits the user of that system, which may or may not be a human being, to use it effectively.

Let us look first at the evolution of hardware technology in two specific areas: general purpose computers and minicomputers. Because user demand differs on these different types of processors, their technology will evolve differently. Minicomputer users, for example, are more concerned with cost than they are with speed. General purpose computer users, while concerned with cost (particularly labor rather than materials costs) are very concerned with performance.

General Purpose Computer Technology

Figure 1 shows two types of integrated circuits. The top circuit is today's technology, the type used in all Honeywell Series 60 general purpose computers. The actual circuit is in the middle of the package, and everything else around it is the packaging that holds the integrated circuit and communicates with other circuits. This is called a dual in-line package because two rows of leads are in line with each other.

The bottom circuit is the next generation of integrated circuit. Of course, it has much more performance and much more density because of the packaging technology of the circuit itself. This particular circuit has six times the capacity and ten times the performance of the circuit above it. This is a good example of what research efforts have done to cut down on delay time, giving a tenfold increase in circuit speed.

Because of process advances such as this, computer developers realize more performance and more density and consequently are able to consistently increase performance in each price range over time.

Micropak

Integrated circuits are combined to build a computer. The circuit is cut out by machine and mounted onto a substrate that is 80 mm by 80 mm, or about 3 inches square. The substrate has pads for mounting the circuit and multiple layers which interconnect the circuits beyond the leads to other substrates. There are no wires. All interconnection is internal.

The substrate shown in Figure 2 contains 64 of the integrated circuits and is equivalent to current 12"-x-12" computer boards in the conventional technology. In other words, this 3"-by-3" package replaces a computer board with the obvious improvements of 16-to-1 area reduction and potential improvements in manufacturing costs.

Figure 1. Two types of integrated circuits.

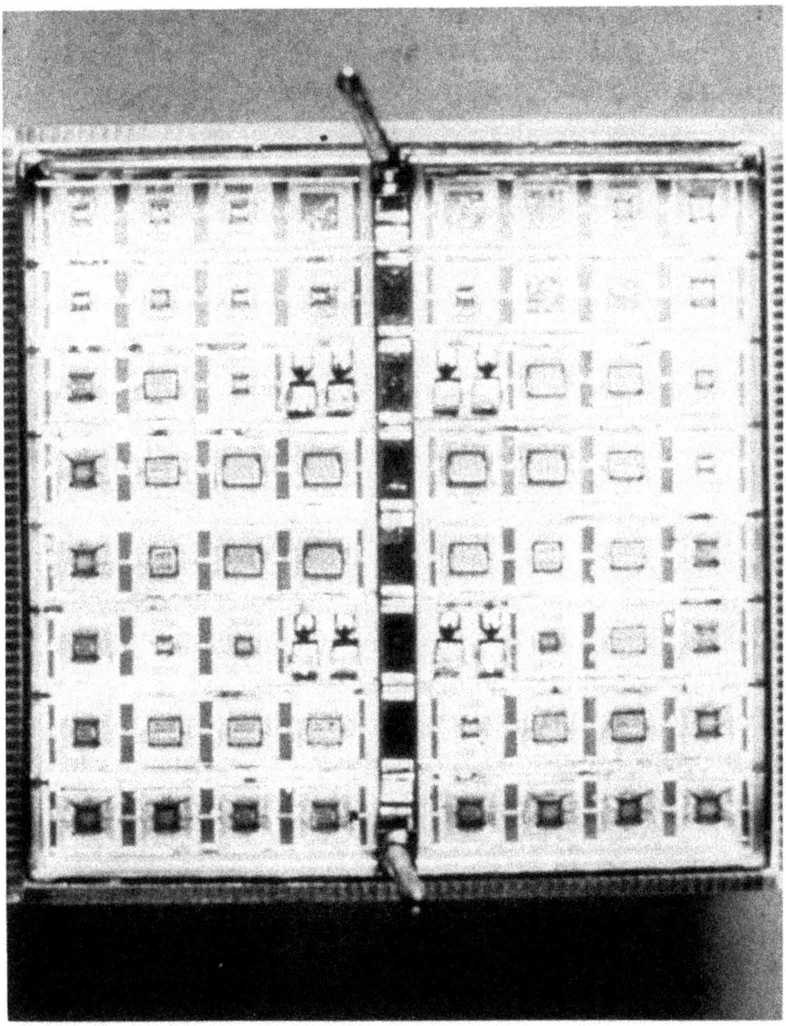

Figure 2. A micropak containing 64 integrated circuits.

The next step is mounting the substrates. Honeywell has developed a new type board complete with connectors to allow the direct plugging in of the substrates. The board accommodates 12 substrates without wiring. All connections are internal, and key lead length is short to speed the travel time from circuit to circuit. Of course such high density circuitry generates a lot of heat and thus requires direct cooling. Honeywell developed a closed liquid cooling system which keeps components cool and ensures good electrical contacts.

For the user these technological developments mean better performance through greater speed and improved reliability.

Primary and Secondary Board Approach

With minicomputers, the object is cost rather than performance since they serve the needs of distributed or satellite processors in networks. Their uses are specialized, and not normally multidimensional as a general purpose computer is. Figure 3 shows a board from the Honeywell Level 6 minicomputer. It is a large board, and the number of components in each integrated circuit is increased to the point where an entire module of the computer fits on one board. The entire central processing unit would be an equivalent board.

Mounted on top of this particular board is another board called a "daughter board." It plugs in and allows one to personalize one board for various amounts of memory or different interfaces. This not only reduces cost in the factory but also allows for extensive configuration flexibility at the user's site.

Megabus and Power Supply

An architectural feature of Honeywell minicomputers that eliminates a great deal of cost and provides a great deal of flexibility is the megabus approach. No matter what is plugged in—memory boards, device boards, processor boards—they are plugged into the same bus, or megabus. The megabus provides the same interface at all plugs. Figure 4 shows a single megabus. Several megabuses can be combined to form the chassis of a

Figure 3. A board from the Level 6 minicomputer.

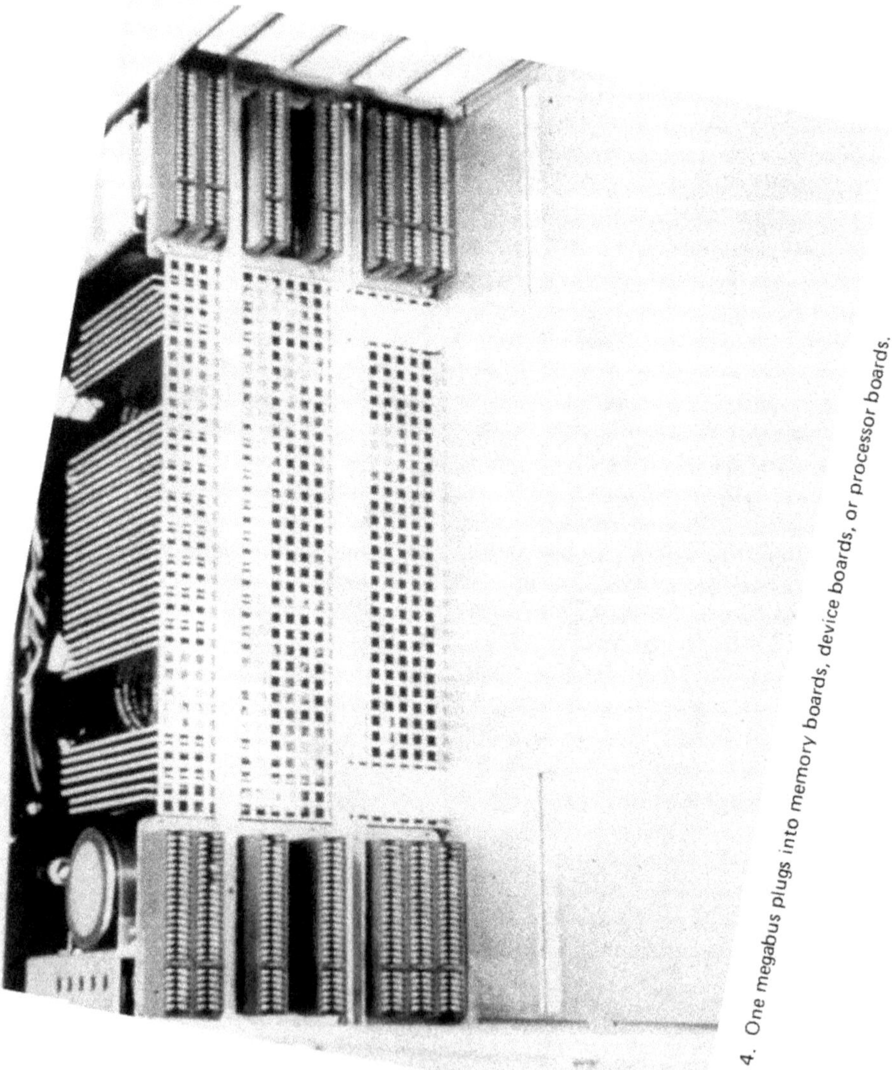

Figure 4. One megabus plugs into memory boards, device boards, or processor boards.

minicomputer, or the basic system components of a large-scale computer.

Minicomputers

Minicomputers are being used more and more as systems components. They are the controllers for networks and peripheral devices, communications interfaces, remote concentrators, the basic intelligence for intelligent terminals, and the basic unit in other component functions in process control types of applications. Future plans at Honeywell include the use of the Honeywell Level 6 minicomputer in many different kinds of applications and functions associated with general purpose computers.

The coordination of the CRT terminal, floppy diskette, and printer with the minicomputer could be used as an intelligent terminal, a word processing system, or even a small business machine with the appropriate operating and application software applied.

The minicomputer is designed to assume many roles. Honeywell is using the Systems Terminal as a key product in what we and the computing world in general consider a very key area in the future progress of computing in business—the concept of distributed processing.

Technology Summary

To summarize the influencing factors of the evolution of hardware technology:

- I see the performance/cost evolution continuing on an exponential curve, typically running 20 percent per year over the last three years.
- Because there will be more power in smaller packages at a lower cost, computers will be able to do things that were technically and economically unfeasible for commercial applications just a few years ago: i.e., the distributed systems approach.

- Computers will be able to utilize less costly memory and circuitry to make things easier from the user interface point of view. A user will spend less time and effort utilizing the power of his or her computer.
- Users will be able to dedicate complete, specialized computers to functions that formerly required general purpose central processor time so that they don't tie up the power of a general purpose machine.

The minicomputer is one of the key elements in future "total systems" architecture. It is the ideal tool for off-loading selected time-consuming functions from the central processor and distributing those functions to the work unit that requires them.

Evolution of Distributed Processing

Now I would like to trace the evolution of distributed systems to illustrate how data processing systems usage has evolved to its present state. This evolution demonstrates a trend toward a systems architecture in which large systems will continue to play a primary, but not autonomous, role, while minis emerge as a key networking element.

The considerations management must face in selecting distributed processing or centralized processing include

- *Costs:* equipment, communications, programming support, and operational personnel.
- *Organizational control:* the degree to which it is desirable to disperse authority to use the computer.
- *Responsiveness:* the relative needs of remote centers for timely access to data versus the needs of the central site for that same data.
- *Security:* the proper level of security for each data element and how it can be maintained.
- *Availability; reliability:* Can the organization afford to have the entire system down, or parts of the system down? For how long?

- *Future applications:* What key applications will be implemented in the future? Can they be better served by a central system or a distributed system? What combination of both?

Keep these considerations in mind as we now review the evolution path.

Years ago, each computer was a single work station in a room where an operator/programmer went to work on the machine. Users would put in their own programs and realize immediate response and total security. However, scheduling one user at a time could not be cost justified, because the processor was idle most of the time.

The next step (and one still very important today) was batch data processing. In such a system many programs are batched and entered to the system all at one time. After processing, the scheduler sequences the results onto an output device. This has proven to be a very efficient form of processing for certain types of applications.

Next came remote job entry to get data to the computer quickly from across town or another state. In this modification of batch, input devices are connected over communications lines. In this manner a central site can serve a remote facility.

The next evolutionary step was time sharing and transaction processing. In the time sharing mode, programmers submit jobs from remote locations and realize immediate response. Transaction processing involves the same type of configuration. However, the people at remote stations are not programmers, but administrative people simply entering data into a data base or getting data from it.

The next step, or more specifically, an alternative systems approach available to users, is to take processing power and distribute it to locations remote from the central site. Many applications, particularly those which relate to the time dependency of transactions, are well suited to this form of processing. It further allows users to choose between the advantages of batch or transaction processing as the specific application dictates. Let us consider some types of distributed processing and what they might do.

A hierarchical system moves from the central systems level in decreasing levels of computing power. At the top level is the central computer. At the next level a remote computer controls a local data base, and, at the user access level, there are intelligent terminals. The remote computers and intelligent terminals can be networking elements made up of minicomputers.

A typical example is the Société Générale system in France, in which the required level of computing power is delegated to central branch area locations. In turn, each local branch has a further subset of local processing power to allow independent processing of customer account inquiries. The central data bases are frequently updated from the remote computers, ensuring that the central files are kept as the master data base.

In a manufacturing environment, the processing power can be distributed to provide local control of such functions as engineering inventory control, purchasing, receiving, and material control. Remote minicomputers can provide local processing as well as interfacing to the host central system.

Distributed system networks can also be structured in a ring fashion where control may be passed from one member computer to another as circumstances dictate. A particular example of this type of network is the planned military defense system shown in Figure 5. Where high availability and flexibility of control are key elements, the ring structure allows for loss of any specific computing element and also for load balancing of the high levels of computer power required.

Distributed Processing User Benefits

Distributed processing provides improved response time. It provides decreased line costs because lines can be concentrated, and data being transmitted and received can be concentrated for high-speed, efficient transfer. Functions better performed at remote sites are off-loaded from the central processor, freeing up the central system. Distributed systems can be configured

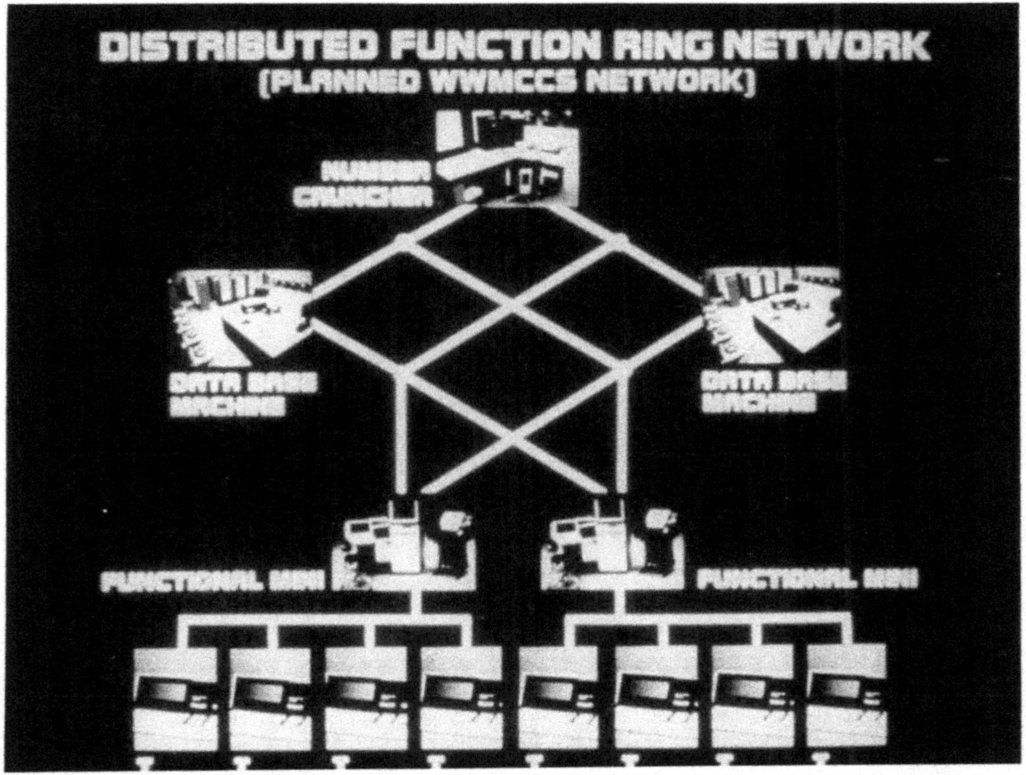

Figure 5. A distributed function ring network.

to provide 100 percent availability, because each element can operate free-standing as well as in conjunction with the rest of the system. Alternate processing paths can be provided for critical applications. Finally, a distributed system provides the maximum in flexibility. It allows the user to decide exactly what capability the system should have and where it should be located.

User Requirements on the Processing Network

Because of this significant evolution of technology (both hardware and systems), the manner in which systems architecture will evolve will be much more directly influenced by the requirements of the system users. Four major requirements will have the major shaping force on the future use of data processing systems: security, availability, flexibility, and ease of use.

Security. Users will have varying requirements for security of their systems, but they should not be forced to pay the overhead price for more security than they require. Future computing systems will provide tools that allow a user to secure a system against unauthorized use and protect data from unauthorized access. They should provide a multilevel capability that allows users personal access to information on the system commensurate with their need to know. Above all, security must be flexible, allowing the users to strengthen or loosen security as the needs of their organizations change.

Availability. Future computing systems must be able to provide the using organization with the level of systems availability it requires. Depending on the organization's needs, the system will be able to provide

- utility equivalent availability,
- alternate path accessibility, or the ability in a network to utilize alternate routes,
- sustained compute power, or the ability through multiple units to have almost continuous "up" time,
- storage redundancy, so that failure of one storage medium does not halt operations,

- graceful degradation, so that, in the event a malfunction does occur, the system itself finds the problem and methodically takes the failed hardware out of operation.

The level of availability required is a function both of the applications a user is processing and the economics of system down time versus additional hardware cost. The key is that the user need only acquire and pay for the availability level he or she demands.

Flexibility. Flexibility is both a general requirement for the architecture of future computing systems and a specific requirement of specific users. Tomorrow's systems will be flexible enough to accommodate the requirements of a broad range of using organizations. At the same time, many users will require a great deal of flexibility in configuring systems to fit their particular organization. Depending on the needs of the various work units in their organization, they will require the capability of configuring a system which is suited to the volume of information being processed, the frequency of demands on the system, and the speed with which information may be processed and results available. They will require flexibility in the power and location of compute units. And they will require flexibility in the size and location of storage units. In other words, the users will tailor their systems and alter them for changing needs.

Honeywell development specifications dictate that the user will have the option of configuring a total system, and that option will span the range from a large centralized batch operation to a fully distributed systems environment.

Ease of Use. If computing systems are to be truly integrated into the operations of colleges and other organizations, use of the systems must be simplified to a point where a minimum of training is required. Two kinds of users must be able to access the system without adapting to a complicated interfacing procedure:

- Users creating and/or entering information
- Users requesting information

Either type of user can be a person or a process. For either, the location of information or the processing required to manage it should be transparent in terms of user consideration.

Requirements on the Vendor

Looking first at the requirements on the vendor in this cooperative effort, the major tasks include

- working closely with the users in the definition and implementation of their uses of large systems in the most suitable architectural environment,
- providing the broad range of products within a solid, clear architectural framework that supports the evolving user requirements,
- providing for protection of the users' investment in today's systems as future systems architectures are being introduced,
- providing the application and system facilities necessary for the computer professional to satisfy the future requirements of the end user, and finally
- providing end user facilities designed to simplify and increase the potential for computer usage in business, government, and academic endeavors.

Requirements on the User

In presenting the requirements on the user, I cannot overemphasize that the driving force of requirements on the vendor is the user's definition and implementation of future information processing needs. In order to perform this task in a cooperative manner the user should

- recognize clearly that his or her needs will be the key determinant in future large systems architecture,
- determine the information systems architecture most suitable to the organizational and business needs of his company,

- work with the vendor in the definition and use of large systems in the chosen systems architecture, and
- understand that the distributed systems-transaction oriented environment, i.e., bringing the processing power and the computer interface to the end user, will further specialize the human resources associated with the computer—end users, application professionals, systems professionals and operations.

Requirements on the Academic World

In order to provide the trained end user and the information processing professionals the opportunity to make all of this happen, the academic world must evolve programs as the requirements of the user are satisfied. In doing so, the following should be considered:

- Computer science professionals will no longer be the primary users of computers! Rather, they will provide the means by which the nonprofessional, the end user, will become the primary information systems interface.
- Increased emphasis should be placed on the nonprofessional's interface with, and use of, the information processing systems.
- The computer professional will further specialize in applications development (working for the end user) or systems/data base management (working in operations).
- The end user will, more and more, become the driving force in the future use of large systems and the processing networks they will host.

Summary

Technological innovation has allowed a distributed systems environment to become economically justified. Minicomputers will also play a key role in determining where and how large systems are used. Computer manufacturers will be reaching for an end-user invisible systems architecture with utility grade availability. These goals can be achieved if, through a cooperative effort, we each do our part. All three participants—vendors, users, and academic institutions—must continually keep in the forefront the requirements of the large systems user and the reality that these requirements cover such a broad range of applications. The principal characteristic in future large systems will be flexibility to allow users to configure the systems architecture that best satisfies their particular needs.

OFFICE AUTOMATION IN THE UNIVERSITY

3

Office Automation in the University: Technical Issues

David Ness

Introduction

It has become fashionable to deal only with issues of grand scope. Often, however, the scope is so grand that the commentary rapidly loses all grounding in reality. In a discussion of technical issues in office automation, participants need have no fear of this happening. Technical issues, although rather narrow in scope, often determine whether systems are accepted or rejected. Indeed, dealing with technical issues often leaves me with the feeling that I'm dealing with problems like those my wife handles in our family: she decides "technical issues" (regarding our daughter's schooling, our budget, and so on), while I make the truly important decisions regarding détente and our perspective on Red China.

What We Have (and Have Not) Found Out

Faculty of the Wharton School of Business have been involved in office automation for more than two years. During this time, they have experienced both the failures and benefits of office automation and have begun to learn (at least a little) from the experience. Here I will discuss some of the things that we have learned, and some of the things that we have not learned during this course of research as well.

Word Processing and Office Automation

Early in the research project at Wharton we decided to separate the notion of office automation from word processing (Ness, 1975a). We decided to regard word processing as an important part of office automation efforts, but not as a major topic of Wharton research. The topic of office automation (OA) is much broader than word processing, although word processing facilities are almost always a part of an office automation system.

Word processing facilities are a part of the OA system at Wharton, but are not emphasized as much as office communication and control activities and office task management. The system is, of course, used to produce academic papers and occasionally to prepare and manage some small mailing lists. Faculty would not claim any particular sophistication for these facilities. They are quite useful, but rather straightforward in their nature. By leaving word processing development to others, Wharton faculty can concentrate development and research efforts on the broader area of office automation.

Early research results suggest that it is important not to narrowly restrict one's view of office automation to only activities related to word processing. Giants in the industry as well as a large number of smaller organizations are currently conducting research on word processing. Since much of the word processing research requires substantial capital investment, it may prove fruitful for nonindustrial researchers to concentrate their efforts in research on other areas of office automation.

Managerial versus Secretarial

A further issue, which is parallel to that just discussed, concerns the focus of energy toward the managerial function of office activities as opposed to the secretarial function. This relationship exists because secretarial activities are quite commonly focussed on word processing, while the managerial function is clearly broader in nature.

It should be clear, of course, that worthwhile research can

be concerned with either the secretarial or the managerial function. Improvements in secretarial productivity can, and no doubt will, be made with technology that now provides opportunities for restructuring secretarial efforts. If faculty exclusively concern themselves with the secretarial function, however, they miss many wonderful opportunities which apparently exist in offices. For example, it may prove, in the long run, to be more important to expand a manager's ability to cope with a new kind of task than to improve secretarial productivity by 10 or 20 percent.

Personalization and History

Investments of the Wharton office automation system to provide personalization and history have been successful. For a description of personalization see Ness, 1976a; for a discussion of histories see Ness, 1976b. These are described in detail in Hackathorn, 1977a. In the personalization system the operation of many programs is tailored to the desires of the individual user. Since an OA system records precisely *who* uses the system (Ness, 1977c), as opposed to recording only an account number, this information can be used to personalize program behavior.

In doing this it is useful to recognize three major dimensions of personalization:

- the "by" user,
- the "for" user, and
- the "terminal type."

The "by" user is the current user of the program. The "for" user is the user for whom the current user is using the program (commonly a secretary using the program for his/her boss). Terminal type determines how much text is displayed. For example, a page full of text is more likely to be displayed at 2400 baud than at 110 baud.

The OA system also keeps two kinds of historical records, active and passive. Active histories can be used to control user interaction in complex program situations. Such histories record whether a user has seen a question before and whether it has changed since the user last saw it. In a system that changes rapidly, such histories can allow users to preserve some semblance of sanity. Passive histories are simply records of use for logging and usage control. By watching which programs and options are used and which are not, system managers can tailor investment in reprogramming and debugging to parallel the interest of the user community rather than relying on unsupported intuition.

Office Processes

While research in the representation and description of office processes is barely under way (Zisman, 1976; Ness, 1977a), some preliminary results are worth mentioning. First, many office processes that appear to be complex on the surface are really a combination of rather simple "remind until done" cycles. Zisman has described the journal referee process, and this process is programmed along with a "request for working papers" process in an APL-based environment in the author's work. Most office processes seem to be simpler in character than these two examples.

Research in the representation and structuring of office processes has also allowed intelligent and unambiguous communication about such processes to take place. In the early discussions at Wharton, different people often took quite different views as to what a particular description meant. However, as such procedures were recorded and described, the descriptions necessarily became unambiguous, and it was possible for faculty to discuss them intelligently.

Impact on Hierarchy

At a conference in New York in early 1976 I predicted that office automation would gradually lead to increasing job differentiation in the secretarial hierarchy. Much of the audience apparently felt that this was social heresy, but I remain firm in that opinion after one and one-half more years of observation. At Wharton, an environment has gradually developed, out of no conscious policy, in which some secretaries know little more than elementary text input while others know how to perform very complex operations. The training staff defined two such roles in their training documentation naturally, and without any suggestion from the research staff.

There seems to be little resistance to the development of a hierarchy from either the secretaries or those to whom they report. Secretaries seem to be quite happy to learn complex manipulations if they are going to use them, and others seem to be quite happy to be restricted to the role of data capture and input.

Less Paper?

One of the most foolish early claims of researchers on office automation is that OA will mean less paper. It seems clear from early efforts at Wharton that any such claims are ill founded. We use more paper than we ever did before. We hope, of course, that we are also making better use of the paper and that our "effectiveness/piece" is way up. Nevertheless, we do use more paper, and any claim to the contrary simply looks ignorant, given our actual history.

It is useful to indicate why mistaken claims such as this one must be dealt with strongly and quickly. Those of us who watched in quiet outrage at the claims made in the early days of computerization remember all too well the disappointment and overreaction which so often followed the discovery of the impropriety of the early claims. Those of us who are interested in having some impact on the practice of automation in the office context must, surely, avoid any hint of this kind of error. False expectations that office automation provides a "solution" to the "paper explosion" are precisely such a danger. It may be good salesmanship (in the narrow sense) to claim reductions in use of paper, but such claims should be viewed with an extraordinarily suspicious eye.

Why do we not use less paper? First, some systems that have reduced volume of paper flow are falsely attributed to "automation." Usually a change in the medium of information transmission causes the reduction in paper use. Automated office systems can work on paper or over direct communication lines. Although there is little reason to expect a difference in paper use on the automated/unautomated dimension, there is much reason to expect it on the transmission dimension.

Second, information is often presented more than once when it proves to be effective to do so. For example, I currently receive about twenty-five computerized mail messages each day. About ten of these can usually be dealt with quite quickly, and they are never committed to hard copy. Of the remaining fifteen, however, about half will be printed once, in my daily briefing, and the other half will be printed twice or more (things that don't get done right away). I could, if paper were my only objective, print all messages once and then cross them off on my hard copy as I dispose of them, but I much prefer to have a new document each day with only active requests.

What Happened to Mail

Observation of the mail facilities of the Wharton OA system (Ness, 1977f) has illuminated another erroneous early assumption. Many faculty found these facilities very important in daily activities, and began to feel that this was a truly superior way to do business. However, early response to the mail facility was naive because the volume of traffic was small. In other words, I had the feeling that I was much more prompt and effective in handling my computer mail than in handling my regular mail. I was correct in such a feeling, but the efficiency was not a result of the computerized nature of the mail. Computer mail was running three to five pieces a day while regular mail was running fifteen to twenty pieces a day. Now my computer mail runs in excess of twenty pieces on many days, and I have become almost as slow in responding to it as I have to regular mail.

I still prefer computerized mail to noncomputerized mail. It is easier to scan, file, forward, and so on. Improvement in handling is not, however, a change in kind, but rather only a change in degree. To claim otherwise is to be shortsighted.

What Looks (Truly) Promising

There are a number of very promising lines of OA research. In each of these cases enough has been done to indicate that further research may prove fruitful, but there is not enough data yet to allow researchers to draw any substantive conclusions.

Almost Regular Processes

In a recent paper (Ness, 1977d) I introduced the notion of "almost regular processes." Although not enough time has passed for there to be much new data on this subject, the technique of looking at office activities as though they were almost regular is very attractive. One department at the Wharton School is currently involved in the process of establishing procedures for the management of the departmental office. In doing this, faculty sometimes needs guidance with respect to the question of whether people will be forced to adjust to new procedures or whether the procedures can be adapted to the wishes of the people involved. While it is quite easy to pay lip service to the notion of serving the needs of the people instead of the system, it often proves to be difficult to do this in fact.

By looking at processes from the outset as though they were almost regular, we find our attention directed toward making sure that we can account for the differences in situations rather than only for the similarities. This fundamental difference in view is guiding faculty at Wharton in directions other than those that we normally would have taken.

Group Attention Management

In a project called GAMS, some faculty at Wharton are beginning some research into the management of "group attention" (Hackathorn, 1977a; 1977b), the process by which a group determines what kinds of problems it faces and how to attack these problems. In GAMS, computer technology is used to experiment with various ways of "managing" the group's attention.

The people whose attention is being managed are regular users of the computer. This is important because the OA mail facility is used to communicate and because the management process often involves the OA system to prepare and deliver a number of documents relevant to the problems at hand.

Wharton's office automation facilities are also used in the GAMS project to store information about tasks that the group is managing. Communications about the status of these tasks are passed through the mail system and these communications, along with other documentation, are periodically incorporated into reports which are ciruclated among members of the management committee.

The Impact of the Hobby World

It is early yet to say much about the impact on office automation of the emerging computer "hobby." The survival of nearly a dozen hobbyist journals is testimony to the number of people who are apparently getting interested and involved in computational activities on a personal level. Although most of the literature, and indeed the current direction of developments in this area, would be regarded as naive by many professionals, it seems clear that it will not remain so for long.

The current thrust of hobby development is the development of BASIC and computerized games, although the first rumblings of "automated letter typing" are beginning to appear in the journals. The terminals used in most hobby systems are small (often only twelve by forty characters for displays or twenty- to forty-character-wide printers), but, if current trends are indicative, terminals will become more flexible and capable. Furthermore, the development of systems that are less prone to failure than the earliest products suggests the growth of interest in a general market other than the electronics hobbyist market. As manufacturers begin to serve the general market, interest in

OA-related activities is almost bound to grow. When this begins to happen, we may expect progress at an extraordinary rate. Even the programming resources of IBM are small in comparison with the potential of one or two hundred thousand hobbyists. Even if only a portion of this programming energy is directed toward word processing and office automation, some dramatic changes will occur in the availability of software and access devices.

Responsive Systems

The emergence of the microcomputer will probably also make OA systems more responsive. It is reasonably difficult to be a "casual" user of a computer system today. Simple things like logging in often require many pages to document when all of the possibilities have to be covered. OA system behavior, when the central computer system is busy or down, when the telephone lines are busy or down, and/or when the terminal is down, provides a number of complicated situations which are difficult for the casual user to keep straight.

Minicomputers can serve as a "turn-key" interface between the user and a complex computer system. Thus, the knowledge required to use the system can be materially reduced, and use of the OA system can pay off much earlier in the usage cycle.

Minicomputers also offer a reasonable prospect of allowing a dimension of personalization quite local to the user. A highly intelligent terminal can be "taught" to allow abbreviations, presentation of data in an idiosyncratic fashion, and other things which an individual system user might deem important. By judicious use of minis, developers may be able to make OA systems more "humane" in their character and thus attractive to a whole new population of users.

Living Plans

The work on "Living Plans" (Ness, 1977e) is a direct outgrowth of the office automation project. Again, although this work is at a very early stage, it seems to be promising enough to warrant attention. Faculty at Wharton have used the living plan process to develop a few working plans and to help develop a course plan for an introductory course. This system involves the creation of some technology to facilitate the preparation of planning documents and the communications that surround the plan.

What Looks (Falsely) Promising

Just as there are some promising lines of research, there are also some lines which, while attractive at first glance, seem generally to prove to be resource sinks.

The Scheduling Chimera

One place where many people try to start with office automation is in the management of personal schedules. Indeed, one of the early parts of the Wharton system (Ness, 1977b) was directed toward this end. This problem is attractive because

- it occurs everywhere,
- it seems structurable,
- it seems "quantitative," and
- it seems that it would have a substantial impact on scheduling meetings.

I am tempted to describe Wharton's efforts in this area as a qualified failure (although some of my colleagues will shout "unqualified, unqualified"). Fortunately, we have had enough successes with our attempts at office automation that we can admit the scheduling failure rather than deny its existence. This failure is attributable to one of two causes:

- the system implemented was lousy, or
- the problems are much more complex than they seem at first glance.

While admitting that the system developed was not perfect, I am nevertheless very tempted by the second explanation. If the OA system was lousy, Wharton faculty who have a lot of experience adapting systems to user needs would have been able to improve the OA system. At Wharton many systems are quite crude (and thus inexpensive) in their first implementation. If usage seems to catch on, then more energy and more resources are poured into the systems to develop them along lines that usage patterns indicate might prove to be fruitful.

There was, at least in the Wharton environment, no such pressure. Maximum usage of the scheduling system rose to three (counting the author) and then ebbed to one (not even including the author). It has remained at this level for more than one year, although many other scheduling facilities have been developed in an attempt to attract some substantial usage. Why should this be the case?

First, it is still easier to carry a small appointment book than it is to carry a computer terminal or other access device. Perhaps if conventional touch-tone telephones were usable as an input and output device, this would be less true, but at the moment it is hard to physically compete with the book.

Second, most people are busy. This means that it is hard to do scheduling well, although it is quite possible to do it badly. When we screw up our own appointment book we are mad enough, but generally we can blame only ourselves or our secretaries. If the computer system screws up an appointment it can be due to the original data capture, the manipulation programs, or the final output preparation process. Such a situation causes the user frustration and quiet rage.

Third, one of the most touted potential benefits, that of scheduling meetings, is actually a detriment to most managers. This is true for several reasons. The process of scheduling a meeting is often a delicate negotiation process, not a simple information transfer. If the president of the United States wanted to schedule a meeting at 11:30 p.m. on New Year's Eve, he could probably get most people to attend, although their schedules might not show them free at that time.

Further, many assume that the difficulty of scheduling a meeting will be materially reduced if information is available.

This is only true if the information is accurate and the schedules involved are relatively loose.

Finally, if knowing someone's availability makes it even one iota more likely that they will be scheduled into meetings, then the system will not be used. Most managers do not perceive themselves as needing more meetings, and a system to accomplish that end is very likely to be circumvented.

In summary, the personal scheduling problem, which at first glance proves to be so attractive, seems more like *Die Lorelei* when viewed closely.

Do It All

Problems in office automation seem best attacked in a "middle-out" fashion (Ness, 1975b). While the somewhat fractionated systems that result from such an approach are occasionally frustrating, they are much more robust than the fragile structures created by the "integrated" approach, which has fallen into such ill repute. Integrated computer systems are fine in a very stable environment where evolution of the system is not an important factor. When change is a normal part of operations, though, most integrated systems are fragile enough to fall apart.

The nebulous notion of integration is to be another of the misplaced objectives which too often attract attention. Until more is known, thoughts of integration generally tend to be steps backward rather than forward.

Economic Issues

While concern for economic issues related to office automation is certainly not disastrous, as it is with the preceding issue, it proves often to be more a source of nattering pedantry than illumination.

Before rushing into the "economic proofs" game, it is worthwhile to consider the use of such arguments at earlier stages of change in the role and function of the office, e.g., introduction of typewriters or dictating machines.

I believe some manufacturers' claims for productivity improvements with dictating equipment, but I also firmly believe that no one either uses dictating equipment, or refuses to do so, for economic reasons. If dictation cost $1,000 per letter (or if it cost $0.00001 per letter), then one would never (or always) use it. However, with cost running within ±50 percent of regular cost, other issues will almost certainly dominate acceptance (setup costs, learning, comfort, and so on).

The same events are likely to occur with office automation. Surely the costs of automation are no longer so great that simple capital constraints will render consideration of automation unnecessary. Further, even if automation causes costs to drop a great deal, users are likely to expand what they do rather than extract the full cost reduction. Although aluminium was more expensive than gold in Napoleon's time, people spend a lot more on it today than they did then.

There is nothing wrong with studying the economics of office automation. It is a shame, though, when people reject consideration of automation because no one can "prove" that they will type their letters more cheaply.

Centralization versus Decentralization

It is also quite tempting to think that office automation will have a substantial effect on important issues like centralization and decentralization of office activities. Except for its impact on the secretarial hierarchy, office automation will prove to be quite neutral in its organizational effect.

Any claims for strong impact on organizational factors at the present time are likely to be just as ill-informed as claims in the late 1950s that computers would lead to organizational centralization. Most computer systems require somewhat different skills than do other systems, but the skills themselves are no more (or less) profound. Some managers will use the control mechanisms which the technology makes available to strongly centralize operations, but others will just as surely use the same facilities to allow decentralization of the decision-making process.

Thus, OA technology is essentially neutral. In fact, of course, most technology is, and it is surprising that so many people are so willing to suggest, often with precious little justification, that "everything is different this time."

Privacy and Secrecy

Research on issues of privacy and secrecy can occupy an enormous amount of time but lead nowhere. Although these issues may be interesting, they are operationally quite separable from most concerns of office automation.

While many managers seem to be quite interested in keeping certain documents private, I have rarely encountered tremendous concern for secrecy, except in circumstances where some formal (legal) requirement demanded it. Most managers seem to be quite willing to accept the kind of security arrangements common in commercial time-sharing operations.

In summary, this and other issues can be deceptively attractive. Once office automation succeeds and some important information gets recorded in the systems, we can begin to worry about this problem. I hope we will be successful enough for it to become a problem.

Data Bases

The notion of an office data base is an attractive one at first glance, but anyone who has ever worked with "consolidated files" knows what a pain this can be. Most "data bases" in office contexts have a number of characteristics that make them weak candidates for the consolidated data bank. First, many of the data bases are small, and the savings implicit in integration are small. Second, most of the data bases are idiosyncratic. Finally, few managers would be willing to relinquish the "control" of "their" data to anyone else, so consolidation is difficult.

References

Hackathorn, Richard D., 1977a. "Research into Group Attention Management Systems," Working Paper 77-07-04, Department of Decision Sciences, Wharton School, University of Pennsylvania.

——, 1977b. "GAMS User Guide," Working Paper 77-08-06, Department of Decision Sciences, Wharton School, University of Pennsylvania.

Ness, David, 1975a. "Office Automation Project: Overview," Working Paper 75-05-03, Department of Decision Sciences, Wharton School, University of Pennsylvania.

——, 1975b. "Interactive Systems: Theories of Design," Working Paper 75-11-02, Department of Decision Sciences, Wharton School, University of Pennsylvania.

——, 1976a. "Office Automation Project: Personalization," Working Paper 76-07-01, Department of Decision Sciences, Wharton School, University of Pennsylvania.

——, 1976b. "Office Automation Project: User History," Working Paper 76-07-02, Department of Decision Sciences, Wharton School, University of Pennsylvania.

——, 1977a. "Office Automation Project: Non-Deterministic Procedures in Office Processes," Working Paper 77-02-02, Department of Decision Sciences, Wharton School, University of Pennsylvania.

——, 1977b. "Office Automation Project: Personal Scheduler," Working Paper 77-02-05, Department of Decision Sciences, Wharton School, University of Pennsylvania.

——, 1977c. "Office Automation Project: On Knowing WHO Uses a System," Working Paper 77-04-03, Department of Decision Sciences, Wharton School, University of Pennsylvania.

——, 1977d. "Office Automation Project: Office Automation Today and Tomorrow," Working Paper 77-07-02, Department of Decision Sciences, Wharton School, University of Pennsylvania. Published as "Special Issue, Office Automation" of the *EDUCOM Bulletin,* vol. 12, no. 3 (Fall 1977).

——, 1977e. "Living Plans Project: An Introduction to Living Plans," Working Paper 77-08-02, Department of Decision Sciences, Wharton School, University of Pennsylvania.

——, 1977f. "Office Automation Project: The MAIL System," Working Paper 77-08-03, Department of Decision Sciences, Wharton School, University of Pennsylvania.

Zisman, Michael D., 1976. "Representations for Office Processes," Working Paper 76-10-03, Department of Decision Sciences, Wharton School, University of Pennsylvania.

4

Office Automation in the University: Administrative Issues

John W. McCredie

Introduction

The primary intellectual activities within universities may be described as the creation, storage, transformation, and dissemination of information. Automated text processing (ATP) systems can facilitate these processes in addition to supporting standard functions usually associated with office automation projects. However, to achieve this broader objective and approach the full potential of ATP, universities should resolve a number of administrative issues that could otherwise limit the impact of this new technology.

The management problems are not unique to text processing systems; most universities face similar situations with departmental minicomputers and other innovations. The differences are the lower prices of ATP systems, the lack of technical sophistication of many of the potential users, and the need for coordination among different departments. The major administrative issues include shared control of expensive components of the total ATP environment (data bases, high-quality devices such as phototypesetting machines, high volume output, etc.), communications standards, pricing policies, equipment acquisition procedures, and centralized versus decentralized management. This paper describes the approach we are taking at Carnegie-Mellon University to integrate text processing systems into the entire university community, the problems we have encountered already, and the difficulties that are waiting around the corner.

The Role of ATP

Sophisticated text processing is related to efficient letter production in a way that is similar to the connection between advanced computing applications and very fast addition and multiplication capabilities. Both advanced areas grew from applications that were valuable, but more elementary and limited. From a solid cost-benefit base, "bread-and-butter" uses mature and spawn new esoteric applications. Modern computers are not just efficient "arithmetic engines," and ATP systems should not be viewed simply as fast typewriters. For example, exemplary state-of-the-art text processing activities, in addition to letter production, include

- manuscript creation, modification, and production,
- electronic mail service,
- teleconferencing,
- integration with administrative applications such as budgeting, accounting, etc.,
- information management of local data bases for mailings, departmental administration, project control, and personnel management, and
- computer managed instructional systems.

These capabilities can support many activities in departments throughout a university. For example, in each of the following typical processes, a well designed ATP system could facilitate effective information transfer:

- Idea generation
- Proposal creation and revision
- Peer review and proposal modification

- Resource allocation decisions
- Schedule generation, modification, and control
- Implementation activities
- Progress and technical reports
- Publication and dissemination of results

There are a number of reasons why universities should investigate the full potentials of these and other applications of ATP systems. For example, a primary educational goal is to train students for future challenges. Since surveys predict that office automation will continue to be one of the fastest-growing dimensions of the data processing industry, universities should pursue research and development efforts in this area. In addition, universities are under severe economic pressure to reduce costs. Educational production functions are labor intensive, and schools have not, in many cases, made use of available technology. The potential benefits of increasing the productivity of faculty and staff by utilizing ATP techniques are great.

The CMU ATP Center

For many of the reasons outlined in the previous section, Carnegie-Mellon University created, in 1975, a centralized ATP Center to coordinate and augment existing decentralized text processing applications. Several departments at CMU need efficient, cost-effective, personal communication channels to large audiences. Increasing secretarial costs make manual methods of satisfying these needs unfeasible. Other departments do not have adequate resources to support increased production of research reports and proposals. Finally, most people at CMU believe that personalized communications in areas such as undergraduate and graduate admissions, marketing of specialized continuing education programs, and fund-raising campaigns result in significant benefits for the university. The challenge to the ATP Center was to take advantage of declining costs of information processing hardware to satisfy these requirements within tight budget constraints.

Administrators considered alternative solutions to the problems. In the area of personalized communication, standard methods such as mass-produced form letters and high-speed computer-printed letters were evaluated. However, the quality of such methods was less than that required by department heads. Increasing the secretarial support staff to cope with increased demand was another alternative, but it was not financially viable.

Initially, the CMU administration supported a small pilot study (1) to determine whether staff should expand elementary text processing capabilities, and (2) to investigate commercially available sophisticated word processing equipment. Following the study, the centralized ATP facility was established. The goal of the center is to increase both personnel productivity and the quality of written communications while reducing costly manual clerical operations.

The initial application, which justified the centralized investment, was the production of many personalized letters for admissions, alumni communications, and post-college professional programs. Departments that use this service have access to university data bases relating to their operations, and they retrieve information from these resources to produce selective mailing lists. The ATP Center has extensive communication links with all university computers. In addition, it has redundant hardware and capabilities to run large production jobs—500 to 20,000 letters—without an operator.

Another standard application is the production of clean drafts and final copies of manuscripts that were created using computer-based text editing systems. Authors often write first drafts at video terminals located around the campus, or at home, thereby avoiding the transcription step. Secretaries then make changes to the copy, stored centrally at the computer center or locally on cassettes. Authors work with clean drafts produced by high-speed printers, and the cycle continues until a final copy is produced at the ATP Center.

Often colleges and universities establish a text processing

center by upgrading hardware in a typing pool or an individual office to word processing equipment. CMU took a systems approach and planned for decentralized expansion by integrating many standard components into a modular system. In the system, computer based text editing and formatting capabilities are combined with data bases, word processing equipment, and other computer resources including specialized programs, disk storage, and high speed printers. This approach resulted in increased capabilities such as personalized mailings to large groups without operator attention, high-speed data transmission among systems, redundancy, and compatibility among decentralized components. When CMU computer center staff were evaluating commercially available subsystems to create the ATP Center, they had difficulty finding vendors who offered equipment with adequate communications capabilities. Most of the systems were designed as stand-alone devices. Now many text processing systems on the market have some communications ability, but buyers must still look carefully to find a system that will support only one protocol.

By starting with a small pilot production system, the CMU ATP Center gave many individuals on the campus a chance to experiment with text processing applications before they invested in departmental facilities. After trying a few different approaches to a text processing problem, they were better able to design a long-term solution that met their unique requirements. This phased approach to development allowed center staff to evaluate equipment from different vendors as they gained experience in solving real problems. The ATP Center leases the systems, although most computing equipment on campus is purchased. Product announcements occur rapidly in this field and center management feels that the flexibility inherent in renting is a prime consideration. As users learn about text processing their requirements change. The ATP Center is always aiming at a moving target. When demand stabilizes, the staff will again evaluate the lease versus purchase alternatives.

During the development phase of the project, the university subsidized the center with an allocation of $7,000. Other expenses were recovered from charges. Since September 1976, the ATP Center has been charging for services on a cost recovery basis and receives no subsidy. However, it does not pay overhead or space charges. The annual operating budget is about $17,000, which includes rental charges for equipment, costs of operating supplies, and salary and benefits for one full-time employee. Users pay for services from the center as they would from office services or an external vendor. In addition, they pay for centralized computer resources from their normal computer budgets.

In March 1977, Carnegie-Mellon submitted a proposal to the National Association of College and University Business Officers (NACUBO) and the United States Steel Foundation for their jointly sponsored Cost Reduction Incentive Awards Program. The proposal "The ATP Center at Carnegie-Mellon University," by Margaret Snyder, documents cost savings to users of about $32,000 yearly. These savings are calculated net of all charges to the center. The ATP project was awarded one of the $1,000 prizes in the competition. Direct cost savings are important, but the major gains will be indirect benefits resulting from more and better communications and the ability to create better proposals and reports.

Current Issues and Future Growth

Five of the six colleges in CMU, a number of administrative departments, and many students currently use text processing facilities at CMU. Rapid growth causes coordination problems. Since the university encourages innovative uses of computers, it is natural for departments to utilize central data processing resources to support text processing. Conflicts arise as educational, research, and administrative users (including text processing users) compete for the same centralized resources. The problems of allocating information processing services to colleges and departments throughout the university are not new, but growth of text processing applications adds a new dimension to an already complex process. Interactive computing, on a month-to-month basis, is two to three times greater this year than last at CMU. Administrators must now account for rapid increases in demand for terminal facilities and centralized disk storage as they plan for computing. Text processing advocates must compete for their share of central facilities. For new computer users who use text processing services only, competition for central computing facilities is a difficult and mysterious activity.

Pricing policies are a major concern in the introduction of any new technology. Since the ATP Center is a cost recovery operation, users evaluate their alternatives and use the service based on rational cost-benefit analyses. An administrative issue at CMU and many other universities is the difference in the philosophy for allocating general computing service from that used for other resources such as the ATP Center. CMU administrators ration central computing service with a mixture of real money transfers for research contracts and selected administrative units and "funny money" allocations for educational and subsidized research activity. Funny money is different from real money because it can be spent only on computing service and because it is easier to get from the central administration than real money.

Problems with this two-tiered monetary system are easy to predict, but hard to solve. For example, early in the fall of 1977, a knowledgeable user printed more than 100 copies of a long technical report on the Computation Center's high-speed printer rather than making one high-quality copy at the ATP Center and 100 reproductions at the campus printing facility. It was easier to issue a print command with a parameter of 100 copies than to arrange for the two-stage process involving the ATP Center. However, the primary reason for this type of behavior is the fact that the Computing Center bill can be paid with funny money, while the ATP alternative would cost real money.

As users plan for new text processing applications, the

computing charging policy causes distorted decisions. Some areas within CMU now have enough text processing work to justify a decentralized departmental computer system with communication links to both the ATP and the Computation Centers. The current CMU budget allocation method discourages a decentralized approach, but for many text processing applications it is the proper technical choice.

At CMU, the University Long Range Planning Committee is evaluating a proposal to move to a real money allocation process for all computing. The advantages are obvious for making decisions about terminals, decentralized versus central facilities, the proper scale of text processing, etc. However, the disadvantages to educational activities, which currently treat computing activities much like library services, are not yet fully understood. The EDUCOM monograph *Charging for Computer Services: Principles and Guidelines* contains an excellent treatment of these policy issues.

Last summer the CMU publications department submitted a proposal to the administration to purchase a computer-based phototypesetting system with text processing capabilities. This proposal focused attention on a number of management problems:

- Is the device a computer (and therefore subject to CMU policies concerning hardware acquisitions) or a composition system?
- How should the ATP and Computation Centers and the publications department cooperate in evaluating, purchasing, and operating this system?
- How should the university charge for documents created and edited using ATP facilities but printed on the phototypesetter?
- Who will create and maintain the new software required to make the most effective use of this new equipment?

The proposal was evaluated under the policy guidelines for minicomputer acquisitions, but communications capabilities for the system were not well defined in any of the technical publications. Purchase approval was given after the vendor committed to support two of the most common communication protocols in use at CMU. At the present time, programmers at the Computation Center are working on ways to transfer text stored in ATP files to the composition system, and users are eagerly awaiting the arrival of this high-quality device.

Conclusion

As text processing grows rapidly at CMU, the ATP Center serves as the focal point for these activities. It recovers costs by charging for services in an environment in which most other computing is purchased with funny money. As users experiment with new text processing applications, they become familiar with basic capabilities. Internal electronic mail usage is growing at CMU, and at least two groups are using EDUNET electronic mail facilities for scholarly collaboration and teleconferencing activities. Cost trends of this new application of computing technology indicate that we are just at the beginning of a period of rapid change in the way people process textual information. We hope that colleges can develop the administrative policies to manage this most recent phase of the information processing revolution.

References

Bernard, D.; Emery, J.; Nolan, R.; and Scott, R. *Charging for Computer Services: Principles and Guidelines.* Petrocelli, N.Y., 1977.

Snyder, M. *The ATP Center at Carnegie-Mellon University.* Pittsburgh, Pa.: Computation Center, Carnegie-Mellon University, March 1977.

5

Office Automation in the University: Reaction and Overview

Thomas M. Lodahl

Elements of Office Automation

First, let's try to clarify what we mean by "office automation." For me, office automation has a number of elements which can be arranged in an ascending order of complexity. People in the field might each produce a different list of elements, but there would probably be a fairly broad consensus on the following ones:

Word processing/administrative support. I put this element first for two reasons: it is the earliest form of office automation adopted in most offices (excepting, of course, computers and copiers), and it is critical to adoptions of higher office automation in that it allows the capture of text electronically. Once the text is put in electronic form it can be transmitted, filed, stored, retrieved, categorized, and otherwise manipulated by computers. Since roughly 80 percent of organizational information is moved around in the form of text rather than numbers, the ability to capture text electronically enables us to apply computer power to text, as has been done with numbers over the last two decades.

Along with automated (i.e., magnetic-memory) typing

usually comes some form of specialization in the office. This means that most, if not all, typing is done in a centralized place. The remaining secretaries (usually termed "administrative") now have very little typing to do, and are thus free to assist principals and other professionals with segments of their work other than correspondence. Since typing is usually more efficient in the word-processed office, some organizations then reduce the total number of secretarial personnel in order to justify the cost of the machines. Other organizations maintain the same number of secretaries, but try to realize their economic benefits by relieving professionals of the more routine parts of their work. In the latter case, the economic advantage can be very high, as professionals usually cost two to four times as much as secretaries. The same also holds true in university environments.

Communications and electronic mail. In the university setting, the possibility of transmitting information electronically—instead of putting words on paper and sending the paper—holds the promise of revolutionizing the whole process of scholarly communication. What it requires is, first, the electronic capture of text, and second, a computer interface with a message switch and/or electronic mail software. But in order to make this work, an entry point is required. Currently, most of the electronic mail freaks I know have their own terminals in their office and do their own keystroking. In my view, very few professors will want to do this in the long run, but in the word-processed office, access to dictation service is usually provided. Once the text is captured through the dictation/transcription process, text can be transmitted through some centralized electronic mail facility. Chances are these would have to be decentralized on campus, perhaps by department. However it is done, the possibility of rapid scholarly communication should provide a powerful incentive for universities to pursue office automation.

Data processing and management information systems. This element of the automated office is already present on most university campuses. However, in my experience access to interactive terminals is still rather limited, and many of us are still in batch processing environments. But any scholar who has extensive data and text processing needs could integrate these services if a keyboard with a CRT were readily available.

Electronic filing and retrieval. Most universities have mainframe computers that are capable of large scale, cheap data and text storage. Again, if interactive access points were available, all of a professor's working papers, data banks, and much of his or her reference material could be stored conveniently in the computer. Through the medium of text editing, text filing, and data processing software, the whole process of scholarly production and revision could be enormously speeded up. Also, the scholar could handle a much wider array of information than at present; in effect, brain power is expanded. A fully automated professorial work station would have to have access to a very sophisticated optical character recognition machine (OCR). This would enable professors to load standard text and journal material, as well as their own writing, into professional work files. Current OCRs have limited ability to read varieties of text, although I am told that this capability is now technically feasible but costly in terms of computing capacity.

Administrative automation. Here I am referring to automation of other office functions such as copying, photocomposition and printing, scheduling, and other office processes that can be more effectively automated once the ability to capture text is present. For example, producing, editing, and printing in-house publications such as catalogs, brochures, and working papers can be done far more cheaply if a word processing origination capability is present. Once the text is captured, it can just as easily be sent to a photocomposer as it can to a scholar a thousand miles away. Those of us who have edited journals will especially appreciate the possibility of this kind of service.

Office automation is a paradigm presently in the process of formation, and many attempts are under way to define the concept and the methods that surround it. To me one of the most useful definitions comes from Harkness in a recent paper,

"Office Information Systems," from the Stanford Research Institute: "Office information systems are inter-active information media that can be programmed to act automatically on their own contents."

University Office Environments

Speaking now as an organizational psychologist, it is my view that most technical problems are at or near solution for office automation, but the human and organizational problems have only begun to be addressed. In the remainder of this paper I will define some of these problems and discuss some of the results of research and development work that my colleagues and I have been doing on this front.

The most important observation we have made is that different office environments require different kinds of automated technical support. What works with one office won't work with another one, and the main task we have been working on is to learn how to specify what kind of technical systems match what kind of office environment. We have been developing "organizational software"—data collection and analysis packages aimed at more precise description of office work environments and needs. Although we have not yet done much research on higher educational organizations, we do have some experience there, and perhaps we can extrapolate some related experiences in other kinds of organizations.

Let us note initially that the university is an ideal site for the application of automated information processing technology. In fact, the major functions of the university can be defined as those of an information processing organization: universities receive, generate, transmit, and store information. The university's reputation is determined by the quality of its research output and by the quality of education transmitted to its students. A system of automation that would enhance these processes would obviously add to the university's ability to survive in today's contracting and cost-conscious economic environment. The economic driving forces toward automating university processes are probably stronger today than they have ever been, but universities have been notoriously resistant to "advances." A number of facets of university organization contribute to this resistance to technical progress.

First, the university is a complex organization which tends to be highly varied across its different departments and other subgroupings of knowledge. This means that what works in agricultural engineering will probably not work in a history department, if only because the agricultural engineers tried it first. It also means that what works in the legal office will probably not help the university development office. Because of its highly complex and decentralized nature, no single automated system is appropriate for the various branches of the university. Each branch or segment of the university, whether administrative or academic, will require its own analysis and its own custom design. It would be absurd to imagine that the typical arts college could be served by a single word processing system, for example. The number of different languages alone would stagger even the most skilled and intelligent typist. So the first task for those who wish to automate the university is to realize that different subgroups require different configurations of service. In turn, this means that office automation in a university must be decentralized.

Second, in many university environments, access to office services such as dictation, typing, and telephone answering often depends on the status of the individual or on his or her access to resources, or both—i.e., having an administrative role, a large research grant, a staff, or whatever. If we now propose to broaden access to these services by adopting office automation, we may run into severe roadblocks on the part of those who have paid the price up to now for access to these services. They will have to be made to understand that even assistant professors still cost about twice as much as secretaries, and that access to services is usually inversely proportional to the need for it. By this I mean that we usually find the junior faculty, who are potentially the most productive of all, hand-drafting or even typing their own papers for publication, while professors and deans typically have more services than they need. In my school, we have just adopted a word processing system with dial-in dictation. The total work load is already at least 150 percent of what it was when the system was adopted, and it is still climbing. This means that work is being done that was not even being accomplished before, and this is typical of our experience in offices when access to services is suddenly given to those who need them. However, privilege always guards itself, and I think we can anticipate skepticism and resistance here.

Another unique characteristic of university environments is that the power to decide on office organization usually resides in lower organizational subunits—departments or schools. If a central administration were to foolishly put out an edict or fiat about the adoption of office automation by departments, it would amuse people, but it would have almost no chance of working. This has meant that equipment vendors have typically thrown up their hands in despair at how to approach marketing to a university. This, added to the fact that university offices are usually not professionally managed—or at worst completely unmanaged—has meant that the vendor marketing representatives have looked for greener pastures than universities. This is not true in community colleges where the president often has enough clout to get anyone to do almost anything he wants. But again, the extreme decentralization and specialization of the large university means that implementation of office automation will proceed piecemeal, if at all.

Finally, university management itself is typically not very advanced technically or organizationally. Office support is often seen as a luxury, and as a cost rather than a benefit. When budgets go down, support staffs are the easiest to cut because they don't have tenure. In a contracting environment, this leaves professionals with even fewer means to get their work done and a decreased ability to survive in their own competitive environments. Many universities still have vestiges of the collegial form of organization, in which faculties participate in the governance of the university. Collegial organization, with its many committees, diffused decision structures, and nonprofessional management, is another aspect of the university environment that will make the adoption of automation difficult. In such environments, the maintenance of values is often considered more important than the cost of doing business, and the result is that the implied value of both professors' and students' time is close to zero.

Strategy Issues in University Office Automation

Despite the gloomy picture I have sketched of the difficulties inherent in the university environment, the advantages of automation are so compelling that it is worth our while to consider some of the specific issues we will face as we attempt to proceed along this path.

First, there is the problem of organizational learning. We have to keep in mind that many parts of modern universities are still technically in the Middle Ages. We can't expect the driver of a horse and buggy to be able to jump into a jet plane and fly it. What we need here are appropriate transitional strategies that allow the department to test the water with its toe before jumping in all the way to automated professorial work terminals. In my own school, for example, we have had to cope with some problems of professorial learning and acceptance of the system, as well as making provision for the support personnel to learn and become familiar and comfortable with the new equipment. Therefore, our communications center has a mixture of correcting Selectrics, IBM Mag IIs, and memory typewriters. Once we have learned to cope with the systems involved with this early word processing technology, we may be ready for a minicomputer-based shared logic system with CRTs, which will allow us to communicate with our main frame computer. Here we are talking about system or organizational learning rather than individual learning curves. Our research experience is that system learning is much less predictable and in general takes much longer than individual learning. I predict that it will require twelve to eighteen months in our current word processing system before all of us are comfortable enough with it to begin thinking about the next step. In general, incremental planning with feedback loops seems to work better than one-shot, total system implementation.

Another strategy issue revolves around the question of cost and benefits and how they are to be measured. In my university, the average professor makes $25,000 a year or more; in a very real sense, the university cannot *afford* to have this person doing very much routine work. With some practice, for example, most people can learn to dictate at least four times faster than they can write by hand; in my view, a major aim for office automation in a university should be to facilitate professional activity and to minimize professional time-wasting. Yet in many universities, professional costs are considered sunk costs, and we only economize on support staff. On the other hand, the introduction of more sophisticated cost-benefit thinking into the university will probably run into severe attack on the part of those professors who feel their time is "invaluable." I would hold that while their time may be invaluable, it is not incommensurate, and that a dollar saved of professional time is just as important and is more costly than a dollar of secretarial time. In other settings, my colleagues and I have been working on ways of getting organizations to be more sophisticated about cost-benefiting professional time; we think these would work in university settings too.

Another strategy issue deals with the choice of an entry point for office automation at a university. Other things being equal, I think I would attempt to utilize some version of Ness' "middle-out" approach. I would probably look for demonstration sites on both the academic and the administrative side of the university, and obviously I would try to pick those that had a good chance of succeeding early on. I would pick them so that once they had mastered the basic word processing technology, there would be the possibility of later adoption of higher forms of office automation. Once they were chosen I would try to make sure that the services provided were at least as good and preferably better than those previously available, especially to junior members. Finally, I would warn them that if they are successful they can expect to be the focus of a lot of attention and visits from other parts of the university.

What Data Processing Professionals Can Do about University Office Automation

First, it is important to keep in mind that data processing as such is only a small part of office automation. In the last ten years, word processing and office automation have developed their own vocabulary, technology, and inner professional structure. Furthermore, although many of the implementation problems are similar between data processing and word processing, the fundamental nature of the beast is different. Data processing deals best with highly structured problems that are susceptible to modeling and analytic solutions; text processing and word processing still deal with messy, "semi-structured information" (Ness' term), which is more complex and less stable than numerical problems. A computer program, once the analysis has been done and the program put into operation, will keep echoing the same thing month after month and year after year; you don't have to keep paying attention to it. A word processing system, on the other hand, is part of an ongoing human organizational process; as the organization itself moves and changes, the system must adapt by noting these changes and by being able to transform itself into something new that will reflect and serve the new conditions surrounding it. The data processing professional who thinks that managing word processing is the same as managing data processing is in for some rude surprises. It would behoove the data processing professional to learn all he can about word processing and its problems before making any commitment to get into it.

One of the big issues among word processing folk nowadays is the question of who will be in charge of the office automation function—the data processing people or the office people?

In the long run, I don't think this is a very important question unless your own job is at stake; whoever is running it will have to know both fields pretty thoroughly, and will have to realize that the problems to be dealt with are organizationally different.

One thing data processing professionals can do right now to encourage office automation is to acquire good text processing software. Here I am referring to the ATMS-Stairs electronic filing system, electronic mail, text editing and text processing packages, and so on. Once these are available on a system, ways should be found to encourage professors and students to experiment with and play with them to explore their possibilities. This might take the form of arranging low-cost or free demonstration periods, providing interactive terminals on a temporary basis for people to try out, and providing personnel and technical support for demonstration projects. In this effort I would encourage you to remember that there are three constituent groups in the university: the administration, the faculty, and the students. Regarding the last, one of my colleagues and I are planning to run an advanced MIS seminar next term in which the students' task will be to develop hardware and software specifications for an advanced student computer work terminal. If the results are any good, we will be glad to share them with others here.

Finally, I think the data processing professional in the university can bring his or her technical expertise to bear in a very important way: namely, by trying to assure some system compatibility between the word processing and data processing parts of office automation. Most of today's stand-alone word processors, for example, have limited communications capability, not only with each other but with main frame computers. The most productive functions of office automation require an integrated word processing–data processing system, and any stand-alone word processor that will not talk to a computer is not nearly as valuable as one that will. I would encourage the data processing professionals to involve themselves in the earliest parts of any feasibility study that may be done, with an eye toward system compatibility. Another area where the technical expertise of data processing professionals can be used is in the attempt to ensure equipment compatibility for downstream growth. The equipment selected for the earliest levels of office automation should be potentially compatible with the downstream, more advanced applications that might be available. By this I mean that today's machines should be compatible with those of tomorrow. They should also be compatible with the peripheral equipment one may wish to add later; for example, OCRs, smart copiers, and interactive terminals. As a psychologist I personally don't know how to do this, but as an organizational analyst I know that these are some of the more important things the data processing professional can do. The automated office in the university will integrate data processing and word processing, and its success will depend on how much each group learns from the other and on how well they can learn to work together.

DISTRIBUTED ACADEMIC COMPUTING

6

Distributed Academic Computing: Technical Issues

R. L. Ashenhurst

To discuss intelligently the technical issues involved in distributed academic computing, it is necessary to have general working characterizations of both "distributed computing" and "academic computing."

Distributed Computing

In the many informal characterizations of distributed computing in the literature and in the trade press, the only point of complete agreement seems to be that distributed computing involves more than one processor. Most often the processors are also assumed to be geographically dispersed (i.e., not in the same room), but a single application being run on several closely associated but distinct processors would be characterized as distributed by some. Others would require that the processors be at least loosely coupled (i.e., via channels, not through sharing memory), and still others would require that common application be characterized at the level of the operational enterprise (e.g., banking), rather than that of the function performed (e.g., data entry).

Most of these nuances arise in discussions of continuing and routine commercial or industrial applications. It appears that to hold to the strict application criterion mentioned above would unduly restrict (perhaps to the point of nullifying) the concept of distributed computing in the academic sphere. On the other hand, since separate applications by independently situated investigators are the order of the day on the campus, the dispersed nature of distributed computing should fit the existing order. This, in turn, implies that processors be loosely coupled if at all.

The reason for coupling is to allow applications to be run on one or several processors, depending on their nature and the variety of services provided in a distributed fashion. Thus, one can argue that a distributed system should be something more than simply a multiplicity of processors connected together. There should be some system commonality among them, which could range from a common communications protocol to full-blown common operating systems support and more, running in one or more processors of the system but available to all. How to specify and design this "something more" is one of the interesting problems in computer systems architecture today.

The term networking has come to connote the interconnection of processor systems through a common communications interface and protocol. "Distributed computing" can consist, in addition, of common or shared services to a nontrivial degree.

An illustration, suggestive but by no means definitive, is given by considering batch versus interactive computing, as these are commonly defined. Sometimes both modes are available in a single processor system, but it has been and may continue to be true that design tends to favor one or the other mode of use. Many universities have thus decided (or been prevailed upon) to obtain a separate system for interactive computing (or for batch, depending on the historical emphasis). If the two systems are placed side by side in a room and run as separate systems, even if external input/output devices can access either system, the result is not a distributed system. If software is provided that allows interaction between the two systems, files to be transferred, and jobs debugged on the interactive system to be introduced into the batch stream, then some form of distributed service is being provided, even though the processors still sit in the same room. The real move in the direction of distributed computing, however, comes when the single interactive system is replaced by several geographically dispersed smaller ones, each of which should still maintain a service relationship with the batch system and perhaps with each other.

Academic Computing

One might characterize academic computing as "that which can be carried out on the computing facilities available on university campuses, or the facilities that someone wishes were available there," and then go on to observe that this includes all kinds of existing computing. Frivolous as this characterization is, it does point up the fact that the diversity of applications in the academic environment is great, probably greater than that of most business or industrial enterprises. Such diversity profoundly influences the nature of the service operation that provides the facilities on which applications are run. Further, although the diversity is great, the volume of one or another application type may be relatively small and tends to fluctuate over time.

Some systematic features do exist in academic computing. The community of academic users tends to be located in one geographically compact area, a campus, or a few such areas, as in a state system. The community consists of a mix of users (professors, students, assistants, etc.) with diverse habits and skill levels, but who are generally above average in motivation and intellectual capabilities. Specific applications of interest to this community tend to have a short- or medium-term life, in terms of programming and reprogramming.

Counterbalancing these specific factors is the great diversity of application needs appropriate to the research and instructional context (number crunching, data massaging, information retrieval, etc.) which typically require any or all of the service modes—batch, interactive, or online.

The inclusion of "online" in this category of service modes is the key to further discussion. The term implies access to computing facilities as an intimate part of a real-world physical or operational process, such as a laboratory experiment or an instructional session. Although in theory terminal access to a centralized system might suffice for such applications, in practice much of the pressure for localized facilities, minicomputers and microprocessors, comes from the increasing importance of online systems as an important variety of academic computing.

To see how online computing needs affect the distributed computing perspective, consider the investigator in a laboratory performing experiments in one of the disciplines of the natural sciences. Part of the experiment consists of data acquisition and either automatic or human-mediated control of the experimental apparatus. For this part of the experiment, direct computer interfacing through a minicomputer and/or a group of microprocessors, has become a state-of-the-art requirement. Also needed, however, is ancillary analysis of the immediate results and various follow-up calculations, perhaps relating the results of a current experiment to previous ones. Such postprocessing activities, as well as the preprocessing activities connected with designing the interface computer programs, are generally carried out much less effectively on the minicomputer system appropriate to the laboratory setup. Microprocessors are even more limited in this regard.

Hence one is led to envision a distributed academic system which combines centralized and localized facilities, the former maintained for general use but providing particular services to enhance the effectiveness of the latter. Many campuses seem to evolve toward such a system without a clearly delineated plan for what kind of a "distributed academic configuration" is eventually to be achieved.

Hardware

The hardware capabilities for achieving a centralized/localized distributed system have been available for some time. In fact, it seems these days that anything can be interfaced to anything, in the physical sense. Costs do vary, of course, and the continuing decrease in the costs of processors and memory makes anything resembling optimization difficult. One very real issue, however, is the degree to which standardization should be imposed locally. The best plan is probably to steer a course between requiring everyone to have the same model minicomputer (this will not succeed in any case) and trying to have a place for every variety on the market. The natural process of minicomputer acquisition on campus, which depends a lot on communication among colleagues, tends to limit the varieties to a few prominent types.

Since even local communication costs can be substantial relative to costs of computing power, the design of the communications system, which necessarily must have considerable standardization, is a separate issue. Transmission rates, the use of asynchronous versus synchronous low-level communication protocols, and the option of a hardwired cable network or the existing telephone system all enter into consideration. The issue of hardwired versus telephone is particularly vexing, since it generally represents a tradeoff between higher initial investment and higher continuing running costs.

A final hardware cost issue concerns distribution of peripherals. One of the advantages of a distributed system is that localized processors can access centralized peripherals, and the latter can therefore be used more efficiently by sharing. In the case of hard-copy input/output devices such as printers, however, there is an undeniable disadvantage in having the device located remotely from the user, and this must be considered in the specifications of the centralized/localized configuration.

Software

The issues relevant to software support for a distributed academic system are less clear than those relevant to hardware. Of course, the software really determines which computing services are distributed by the system and indirectly determines the ease with which the user can take advantage of them.

The minimal system software that must be supplied for a distributed system is the network control program. The network control program implements so-called low-, intermediate-, and high-level communication protocols. In other words, it monitors respectively the hardware interface, the device driver software, and the software that uses device drivers for transmitting data in aggregates such as messages, files, and programs. These protocol levels are distinguished in the ARPANET, which is the prototype for much of the general network technology as it exists today.

In ARPANET, the low-level control programs run in intermediate "node-interface" processors (IMPs), one associated with each processor (node) on the network. However, there is no reason in principle that such programs cannot be incorporated in the higher-level network control programs that run in the (networked) processors themselves. This conceptual framework extends to smaller local networks, of the type underlying the distributed systems under discussion here, and several vendors have announced packages for networking minicomputers of the type they produce. Use of vendor-produced network control devices for mini networks has the possible disadvantage of not allowing free choice of processors to be incorporated in a distributed system. The practice also tends to introduce a lot of communications overhead, which may be necessary for a pure network system to function reliably, but which can be absorbed in other software if more general distributed operating system functions are supported.

Such functions are realized in one or more but not all of the processors of a distributed system. Thus, it is possible to have many of the smaller units, i.e. minicomputers, run with an internal operating system that is minimal compared to what it would require if it were a stand-alone. Standard functions, such as file handling, editing, and program development, are then available on a centralized basis. The use of remote peripherals by minicomputers is also handled in this way.

Systems

The overall design issue then becomes a macro system one—how to formulate the capabilities desired in terms of transfer aggregates (messages, files, programs) and system sites (e.g., where user programs are stored, processed, executed). In the optimum system, the individual user has access to the widest possible range of capabilities, while at the same time the use of resources shared over the whole system is balanced. In other words, the normal operating system problem is applied to the extended distributed system configuration.

A secondary, but nonetheless important, issue is the extent to which the distributed nature of the services should be transparent to the user. Although there has always been sentiment in favor of the idea that the user should just know that data is stored, without being concerned with where it is stored, in a loosely coupled system the idea of different sites of activity does become practically important (e.g., one site may be down, another up). It should not unduly tax the patience of the user to have to take this into account, as long as dealing with the distributed structure is smooth and flexible.

One way to permit centralized facilities to be shared as an adjunct to localized ones is to have a hierarchical organization, with higher levels in the hierarchy representing greater degrees of sharing. Although this type of organization usually applies to hardware (the interconnection diagram is a tree), it is just as appropriate for software. In fact, the partition of a (symmetrically interconnected) network into "provider" sites and "user" sites, if strict, would give a two-level functional hierarchy. This concept has been formulated in connection with the ARPANET (as service and user sites), where all the nodes are physically at the same level.

One could realize a functional hierarchical system by having a general communication network connecting all facilities, and let software protocols define the mode of service obtained by user systems (minis or micros) from provider systems (generally maxis or midis). Alternatively, one could have an intermediate level in the hierarchy, a system designed specifically to connect user sites (minis) to provider sites (general-purpose maxis) and supply a limited range of services itself. If intercommunication among minis is desired, it could be controlled through the intermediate level, making unnecessary a general network (where every site can communicate directly with every other). The resulting network displays a rather different physical organization, with maxis at highest level interacting with minis at lowest level via the intermediate level, which is the "heart of the system."

The design issues for such a system are: what services are supplied at the intermediate level (including accessing services to the highest level), and how is the choice made between general services and services that are mini-specific or maxi-specific?

The MISS project at the University of Chicago uses a network of the three-level type. A PDP-11/45, configured as a midi with file and I/O peripherals, functions as the intermediate level. It is dedicated to the mediating task, and is designed to take over as much as possible the function of facilitating the use of its services and those of the highest-level service system (the campus general-purpose computation facilities) by the lowest-level users (individual minicomputer sites). The intermediate-level system supports general varieties of minicomputers (currently PDP-8s, PDP-11s and Nova 800/1200s) and connection to a variety of general-purpose facilities in such a way as to require as little specialization of the minis or the maxis as possible. Currently only the Computation Center 370/168 functions as the general-purpose facility.

A useful way to envision the relation of intermediate level to the minicomputer here is to think of it as a nonresident operating system with built-in communication to general-purpose facilities. The minicomputer operates effectively with a minimal amount of its core dedicated to the low-level protocol for communication with the intermediate level. Currently, software for the communication function occupies approximately 1.3K words of core on a PDP-11 or a Nova 800/1200. If the minicomputer is run with its own operating system it must, of course, be modified to include the communication protocol within it. Such a modification is a possible source of complication since one must have some specifics for each possible operating system, not just each minicomputer variety.

To the highest-level system, the intermediate level appears to be just a front-end, communicating through a channel and acting like a conventional remote access facility (e.g., terminal or remote job entry station).

The MISS architecture succeeds fairly well in leaving specifics either to the lowest level, which is user programmed, or to special software at the highest level (e.g., cross-assemblers, which must ultimately produce code for a specific minicomputer). One hybrid form of support exists, where a minicomputer runs its own specific assembler but uses the intermediate-level file system for its source and object program repository.

An attractive aspect of the hybrid system is the possibility it affords of sharing expensive peripherals such as a printer. This is naturally realized in the nonresident operating system concept. The inconvenience in having printer output produced at a physically remote location is partially alleviated if data concentrators are placed at locations near several minicomputer sites and the peripheral capabilities of the support system may be replicated.

An important goal of the data concentrator design is to present the minicomputer user with a set of options on the localized/centralized spectrum. Options can range from completely localized (in which case the minicomputer operates as a stand-alone) to completely centralized (in which case the minicomputer operates as a terminal to the higher level systems). The extent to which the services are utilized can vary from site to site, and the spectrum of utilization is in a sense "market determined."

The issue of how to structure intermediate-level services is a more complex version of a problem that arises in a pure network (communication services only). The use of separate node processors (like the IMPs of ARPANET) is an intermediate level, in the sense described here. One could consider transferring some of the services now contained in the network control programs of a pure communications network, which run in the main (networked) processors, to the node processors. This arrangement is counter to the possibility, already mentioned, of putting all the interface processor capabilities into the network control programs.

If one chose to design a hierarchical support system with no explicit intermediate level, in the result one could probably distinguish a "virtual intermediate level" contained in the operating systems of the computers involved (the providers, the users, or both). The intermediate level would consist of the software that is dedicated to supporting the interaction of the producer-user relationship and that is commonly available (symmetrically) to all user computers.

At the moment, MISS involves only user minicomputers, and they communicate only with the intermediate level. Features allowing interaction of these minicomputers with one another and permitting some to act as provider components (and hence to become service "back ends") are possible under the basic three-level hierarchical design.

Experience with MISS, as the system has grown, has been favorable. There have been minicomputer users connected to the system for three years, and charges for the intermediate-level services for two. The minicomputers have put the system to many and varied uses. At the later stages of system design, several features were incorporated that had been requested by users. MISS experience has effectively demonstrated the importance of having a basic framework design for the intermediate level that is solid and reliable. Further, the intermediate-level design should embrace essential file and communication features but permit further introduction of support packages (such as editing, etc.) at both intermediate and highest levels.

Perhaps the most important conclusion drawn from experience with MISS is one which is only quasi-technical. Because the project concentrated on intermediate-level architecture, the project staff became dedicated, in the human sense, to the idea of minicomputer support. They played and continue to play a mediating role between the minicomputer users, who are oriented to their applications, and the Computation Center providers, who are concerned with general applications of all types for the whole campus. Now an identifiable staff serves the constituency representing online applications which, as already stated, are the key ones for the concept of distributed academic computing. From the point of view of both the project and minicomputer users connected to MISS, the availability of this staff is one of the chief advantages of being part of the system.

7

Distributed Academic Computing: Administrative Issues

D. C. Spriestersbach

An Administrator's Perspective

Feelings of dread are typical of the emotions that many university administrators feel when they confront issues involving computers. For most of us, computers were something with which we had little or no intimate experience until we became administrators. For a large number of us, and for a larger number of our faculty colleagues, this innocence about computers persists.

Often the place of libraries as an integral resource within the academic community is well accepted, even unquestioned, while the place of computers is unquestioned because it is unrecognized. (This kind of attitude has generated a problem with an ironic twist; we enlarge at great cost our facilities to store books despite our growing facility through computers to store the information they contain in a form which can be more readily accessed, shared by a greater number, and at substantial savings.)

Yet the insistent thrust of computer technology upon the academic scene has forced academic administrators to get involved in agonizing questions related to computers that require the reordering of traditional priorities in the allocation of finite resources; and, as a consequence, to become embroiled in issues which create consternation and disbelief, and even polarize university constituencies. Administrators must also serve the great mass in academe who seem not to care whether computers exist. Among the members of this group the assumption is made that somehow God will provide. For them, administrators must become evangelists—spreading the gospel that the vitality of the faculty and of educational programs can be significantly inhibited or enhanced by the absence or presence of up-to-date computer technology.

I know very little about the technical aspects of computers. I know very well, however, that computers cost a lot of money. During the twelve years that I have had the administrative responsibility for the development of the University of Iowa's computer resources, I have also learned that computing is a rapidly developing, fluid technology, and that there are always a variety of legitimate strategies from which an institution can choose to respond to constantly emerging developments. I have learned that to be a responsible administrator, one must make a selection and work for its implementation regardless of one's dearth of expertise in the complex field of computers. The effective administrator cannot afford to react to issues as they arise in this fast-moving area. Moreover, he or she must be supra-active within the political system of the institution, vigorously espousing the cause. Because of administrators' lack of knowledge, they present the case for computing largely on faith and, because of similar lack of knowledge, their constituencies must accept the case for computing on faith as well. For the administrator, that faith is usually derived from the trust that he or she has in the capabilities of professional computer people on campus.

What follows stems from my particular background, my specific academic administrative assignments, and my peculiar biases concerning the place of computers within the educational process. I must leave discussion of the technical aspects of distributive computing to the experts.

The University of Iowa Context

A brief description of the computer facilities at Iowa may give readers some feeling for the context of the following remarks. The University of Iowa has three main computer systems on campus. They are associated with Data Processing (located in the offices of the vice president for finance), the University Hospital Computer Center, and the University Computer Center.

Data Processing is equipped with an IBM 370/155 with modifications to make it essentially equivalent to the 370/158. This unit handles the needs of personnel, payroll, purchasing, admissions, the registrar, and university accounting and finance. In addition, it has a number of data display terminals hooked to the computer channel that are distributed in various offices, including those of the deans of the several colleges. These terminals allow visual access to a variety of records maintained in the system. Use of this system is characterized as being heavily file oriented and demanding great regularity, security, accuracy, and timeliness. It is a totally closed environment with no user programming allowed in the system.

The University Hospital's computer system consists of an IBM 370/158 operated in an online, real-time interactive style with great reliance on files. Again, great emphasis is placed on accuracy, security, and real-time response concerning patient records. It, too, operates in a closed environment and employs primarily a single language.

The University Computer Center is equipped with an IBM 360/65 configured with a wealth of peripherals. In addition, there are four Hewlett-Packard 2000 series units used to drive the terminals in our minicomputer centers. These centers are primarily for instruction but we have, in cooperation with Hewlett-Packard, developed the software which enables us to access the 360/65 through the HP units so that these terminals can be used for complex research jobs as well. We also have a hookup with the Iowa State University computer for sharing programs and data and for off-loading large batch jobs, and we provide the administrative and academic computer support for a regional computer network consisting of one Iowa public school and fourteen colleges in eastern Iowa and western Illinois.

There are also approximately eighty online, dedicated minicomputers associated with the work of particular laboratories. In addition, the Department of Physics, which is deeply involved in space research, has three UNIVAC 418 systems and three CDC systems (two 1604s and one 3800). Both systems are used primarily for real-time data gathering and subsequent data reduction and analysis.

In August 1976, a CDC CYBER 70 Model 71 system was added to the University Computer Center system. It has a current capacity for sixty-four terminals, which may be cathode ray types or keyboard/printer terminals. The CYBER also has access to the IBM 360 through a facility called TIELINE.

The relatively large number of minicomputers on campus is a result of specific academic strategy. In 1973 academic administrators at Iowa decided to make computer technology available in a systematic way to our educational programs. We now have approximately 200 terminals (keyboard/printers and cathode ray tubes) located in various colleges and departments including business administration, education, engineering, political science, mathematical sciences, pathology, drama, and the language lab. And the demand continues to grow.

Thus, we started with a central facility designed to meet the research needs of our faculty and students. We controlled its development by requiring that all requests for computer equipment be reviewed by university computer committees to ensure that the equipment being purchased by departments was to be used exclusively as online laboratory controllers. (Making such judgments is not easy because many pieces of equipment have data handling capabilities even though they are designed primarily to do other things.) The university has now moved to a distributive system. The hierarchy of computers will ultimately be able to serve both the instructional and research needs of students and faculty largely through terminals located close to their classrooms and offices.

Administrators at Iowa are painfully aware that the IBM 360/65 which serves as the primary batch computing system is obsolete. We have been able to maintain the capabilities of the system at a reasonably adequate level up to this point only as the result of fine tuning and front-end modifications by a skilled and imaginative staff. Its replacement and a funding arrangement that will allow us to keep abreast of technological developments in the future is currently one of the highest priorities of the University of Iowa. The faculty and staff are currently beginning, for the second time since I assumed my present administrative position, a university-wide review of all of our computer systems to see if present arrangements should be modified.

The introduction to a paper titled "Requirements for Distributed Computing Systems, 1980 and Beyond," by Distributive Computing Task Force of SHARE (August 1977), includes these comments:

> Distributed computing is the logical and/or geographical dispersion of computing nodes, interconnected on a coordinated basis. The interconnection must be such that a single logical set of computing functions is split among multiple physical devices, with each doing a portion of the total computing required.
>
> Distributed computing is a hybrid between centralized and decentralized approaches. It is not a panacea, but does have the potential for many applications. To realize its potential, a total, uniform distributed system must be produced.
>
> Most computer installations would claim these two objectives: (1) the efficient and effective utilization of personnel and computer assets and (2) the provision of a high level of service, at a low cost, for a wide variety of applications.
>
> Unfortunately, these two objectives are often in direct conflict. Centralization, while achieving economies of scale and more standardization, has usually resulted in reduced accessibility and degraded service for individual users. Decentralization, while providing rapid and individual response to local needs, often

leads to redundancy, lack of standardization, lack of control, and inaccessible data.

Our need is a distributed system which will be flexible, and most important, easy to use. It must combine the advantages while minimizing their disadvantages.

In my judgment, administrators at the University of Iowa have been aware of many of these considerations as we have developed our system. We have identified distinctive administrative and academic needs and dedicated computer resources to them. In doing so, we have chosen multiple types of computers and multiple vendors. In addition, we have allowed a modest dedication of technicians, programmers, and shops. We have recognized that rising costs can be minimized through sharing with Iowa State University, the institutions in our Regional Computer Network and, most recently, by our decision to bring TYMNET access to the campus. In sum, to the limit of our resources we have taken the computer to our faculty and students. Moreover, we have attempted to improve the accessibility of the computer to these units through the efforts of the Users Services unit of our UCC whose personnel daily "circuit-ride" the campus, identifying the needs of our people and attempting to match these with available resources.

Where Do We Go from Here?

In thinking about the future I, as a university administrator, have made the following assumptions:

- *Computers are here to stay* in the academic scene; their use will continue to grow both in research and instruction.
- *Computing will continue to creep into other technologies,* largely in "hidden" micro forms through such items as typewriters, video units, and photocomposition equipment, to name but a few.
- *Communication methods will be refined,* involving such technologies as microwave, infrared, light fiber, and

satellites, to the end that even more distributed computer services will become realities.

- *Distribution will involve not only data sets, in the pure sense, but also improved voice communication,* image communication, and facsimile communication.
- *Resources available to higher education will not increase beyond the inflation rate.* However, there will be major reallocations to accommodate to new educational delivery modes in response to refresher/recertification courses, continuing education opportunities involving lifelong learning programs, and the growing extension of the concept of campus to remote locations.

To the degree that these assumptions are valid, I predict that the justifications for distributed computing will increase and that distributed computing arrangements will grow in number. If I am correct, we will need to make some improvements in our management processes. Certainly, as always, the resources that will be available to us are going to be limited. We will accommodate to new needs largely through internal reallocation, a painful process. Clearly, if our computing needs are to command in the future a relatively larger proportion of our resources, we are going to need a strong and clearly rational basis for deciding what the nature of computing facilities should be and where to locate them to maximize their impact on our instructional and research programs.

None of us is now prepared to make the hard defenses necessary for our changing and increasing computer needs. Furthermore, the professional computer people on our campuses will not be able to carry the day without the constant and stable support of central administration. For involved here are issues related to the missions of institutions, student body mix (resident, off-campus, part-time, lifelong learners, undergraduate, graduate, professional), and the relative emphasis on teaching and research. Involved also are universitywide efforts to evaluate teaching and learning effectiveness with particular reference to possible changes that computer technology would be likely to make in assuming a more expansive and pervasive role in the teaching and learning process. Necessarily then, we will have to involve faculty, students, and administrators in an increasingly intense, descriptive, and evaluational institutional analysis that will enable us to make better forecasts of where we want to be and when we will arrive there. No institution can simply take a computer off the shelf and plug it into the educational system, even if it could afford to do so. Computers, to be used effectively, require as a prerequisite sophisticated and complete planning on an institutionwide basis. In my judgment we are far from that stage now. It will take strong leadership at the very highest levels to institute the kinds of wide-ranging forums and institutional reviews that will make long-term significant future changes possible.

We will have to face several specific issues as we move increasingly into the distributive mode.

We will need an adequate degree of compatibility among distributed units to ensure reasonable interchange between them. Therefore, we will have to develop guidelines that indicate when we will require compatibility and when we will ignore the issue.

We will have to identify the nature and level of controls that should be imposed on the requirement of transportability of ideas in the form of programs and data. For example, unless data units are appropriately basic in the growing number of statewide data pools, these pools will have greatly restricted use by researchers with varied interests and backgrounds.

We will have to assess the amount of redundancy properly allowable in maintenance contracts, technicians, shops, and programmers as a result of our policy of using a variety of computer hardware and software to meet our various needs.

We will have to determine the appropriate level of merged services for computing with other academic service units such as the library, audio-visual unit, graphics, photo services, and printing and publication services. The boundaries of the activities of these individual units are becoming increasingly blurred, yet we have done very little to explore how these units should be combined and managed.

We will have to define more precisely the nature of proper exchanges between academic and administrative computer units. Must administrative systems be totally closed? Are there not ways to access the data in administrative systems for research purposes that will not violate security, privacy, and timeliness requirements?

We will have to move toward a balance of payments for on- and off-campus computer services. Clearly there are times when we can profitably purchase computer services off campus. But our fiscal resources are finite, and I assume that we will always need an on-campus computer facility of some sort. What then are the adequate bases, controls, and mechanisms for controlling the use of off-campus facilities by on-campus constituencies?

We will have to reassess the role of the central computer resource. The time is rapidly approaching when the academic computer center that has the only identifiable computer facility and staff on campus will be a thing of the past. What then will be the nature of the central unit? Will it become only an information warehouse containing volumes of data and the software to make them available for distribution elsewhere on campus?

We will have to plan and establish administrative structures for effective institutionwide computer management. The growing potential for interactions between computers may make it necessary for institutions to have computer czars responsible to the highest levels of central administration for computer facilities and computational activities. This concept is not necessarily incompatible with a move to decentralized computing. In fact, to avoid great inefficiencies and organizational chaos as a result of distributive computing, the establishment of the czar may become a necessity.

We will have to improve administrative evaluation processes for computers and computational activities. Although many may believe, as I do, that computers are a cost-effective technology in terms of their impact on the quality of university teaching and research, we will not be able to avoid the fact and the charge that computers remain a very high-cost enterprise. If a significant reallocation of resources is to take place within our institutions to accommodate to computer advances, administrators are going to have to improve significantly their efforts to justify the cost of computing. Our best efforts to date are largely anecdotal, and testimonials are simply not going to be enough in the future to overcome the universal challenges for dividing academic funds.

Finally, we will have to determine the appropriate sources for budgeting distributed computing. Should these facilities be financed centrally, as libraries are, or should they be built into the budgets of the user units at least to some degree? In the early days of academic computers, the units were used primarily as instruments in support of research, and their costs appeared among those assigned to research. Today, even though these facilities are used increasingly for instruction, their costs continue to be charged largely to research. This may be a strategic error if administrators and faculty expect an increasing proportion of institutional budgets to be devoted to computing.

In addition to the costs directly associated with computer hardware and software, resources will also have to be identified and allocated to provide spaces for the distributed units, to secure the equipment distributed, and to supply personnel to assist in its effective use.

In my judgment, universities will be in a much stronger position to accomplish these objectives if departments and colleges are involved in providing partially for the financial support of distributed units. The day is past when institutions need to provide these resources totally from central funds. The assumption no longer holds that such provisions are necessary if administrators want the technology to be tried and subsequently integrated into the teaching and research of academic units. Departmental contributions were deliberately required at the University of Iowa, and the procedure worked far better than expected. By now, the importance of the technology for our teaching and research is well enough established that it can be expected to move ahead on its own merit and with its own momentum.

Finally, and not inconsequentially, unless administrators find ways to relate computer costs appropriately to teaching and research, they will mislead themselves, those who review budgets, and those who support them in debates about the true costs and needs of each activity.

8

Distributed Academic Computing: Reaction and Overview

John E. Skelton

Introduction

"Distributed computing" has become a popular industry buzz-word over the last few years. As with most buzz-words, there are differences of opinion among users of the term regarding what is actually meant. Perhaps it is best to start with a definition of the term.

In a recent publication of the National Computing Centre of the United Kingdom, Down and Taylor (1976) offer the following prerequisites for a system to be termed distributed:

- processing ability physically located at more than one location
- utilization of that ability for user-oriented tasks
- interconnection of the locations through some form of data communication facility
- existence of a data handling facility at each location, although not necessarily data storage at each
- observance of common standards in the use of the facility at each of the locations

Reporting on a WESCON 77 session on distributed computing, Wiseman (1977) noted the definition in use at the session:

> a variety of processing structures whose common goal is the placement of local computing power at the disposal of every unit . . . for the purpose of enhancing each unit's operations and controlling a timely flow of intelligence among the units.

Although both were speaking of distributed computing in a commercial environment, it seems clear that distributed academic computing is not very much different. I offer the following three essential characteristics of a distributed academic system:

- multiple locations of processing capability tailored to meet the needs of a high percentage of the local users
- a user transparent communications linkage between locations so that the user needs that cannot be met by the local capability can be met by facilities at another location
- a high degree of software compatibility between all elements of the system so that transport of software between locations can be accomplished quickly and effectively

Distributed versus Networked Systems

One is naturally led to ask the question, "What is really new? Isn't this what networking is all about?" The most publicized network, ARPANET, appears to meet all of these definitions. Down and Taylor (1976) offer a succinct distinction between distributed and networking systems:

> In networking systems the objective is to transport tasks efficiently to an optimum processing resource which is not usually sited at the point of user activity. By contrast the objective with distributed systems is to process as many tasks as is economically possible or administratively desirable, at the point of user activity.
>
> Networking takes the job to the processing resource; distribution takes the processing resource to the user.

The distributed computing concept is an extension of networking technology in which a large number of processing tasks, rather than being forwarded electronically to a large-capacity processing resource, as is the case with most networks in operation today, are processed at the end user location. Only tasks that do not fit the design of the local system are forwarded to another processing resource, presumably a resource with higher capacity and more flexibility. The dramatic increase in mini and micro systems' price-performance ratios and capability has made this possible. Moreover, much of the communications technology that makes distributed systems possible relies heavily upon the already implemented technology of networking systems.

Advantages

Distributed systems offer advantages and disadvantages to the academic user. Down and Taylor (1976) suggest that the following advantages may be derived from distributed systems:

- increased flexibility
- improved utilization of resources
- improved service to users
- simpler systems design
- improved security
- greater human involvement
- improved capability for control

Considered in an academic environment, these advantages can be grouped into three areas for discussion: (1) reaction to user needs with subheadings of capability and flexibility, (2) resource utilization, and (3) systems design.

It can be argued that distributed systems offer a greater facility for meeting end-user needs than do conventional systems. Because computing power can be located at points of high user activity, the needs of the users at these locations can be more effectively determined and a processing capability to locally meet a large percentage of those needs can be made available. Communications to other facilities can provide for those needs not met by the local system. Thus the computing capability available at each location can be quite varied when configured so as to meet local user needs. The size or scale of the local processing capability can also be adjusted to a considerable degree so as to meet changing requirements.

Distributed systems appear to offer the prospect of a higher level of resource utilization. All sites do not need large or unique resources for only a small percentage of the users if such resources are available to the users who need them through the communications network. Incremental costs to serve what seem to be ever-growing computing needs can be relatively small, since local systems can be configured and sited to meet these needs as they arise.

It can also be argued that distributed systems offer the advantage of simpler systems. The hardware-software interface is simple and the end user needs only a small amount of systems knowledge to effectively use the total system. When systems are tailored to meet high-volume local needs, complex systems designed to accommodate all possible users will be less necessary. Because of less complex systems and a more specific hardware implementation, the control language can also be much simpler and hence easier to learn and use.

Disadvantages

What are the disadvantages? It has been argued that distributed systems offer access to computing resources at a lower unit cost. However, the potential savings can be realized only if the institution is already in the process of replacing a large central system. In most cases the large central facility represents an equally large investment of capital funds. Additional funds are not going to be obtained easily unless the central facility is already in need of replacement or extensive upgrading. The cost savings that seem to be implicit in the utilization of mini and micro technology may be more than offset by the cost of replicating software, data storage, and the increased maintenance costs of geographically dispersed systems.

Another problem is resistance to change from entrenched computing forces. As noted at WESCON, "disturbing the calm of the 'old regime' may be disastrous" (Wiseman, 1977). A change to provision of computer resources via distributed systems would necessitate a change in the organizational structure of computing on many campuses. Support staff in the form of user services, operations, and maintenance would necessarily be quite different. In a conventional computer center, these are the units most visible to the end user and thus most sensitive. In a recent study, Chambers and Poore (1975) recommended that load-sharing networks be limited to a geographic radius of 50 to 75 miles because "beyond these distances, transmission charges, personal calls and visits involved with overall administrative matters as well as day-to-day procedural problems become too costly, time-consuming, and generally annoying." Load-sharing networks are not quite the same as distributed systems, but, having had experience with academic use of widely dispersed systems, I can attest to the fact that the issues are germane.

In distributed systems, systems and languages must be compatible. Chambers and Poore (1975) recognized the importance of compatibility when they noted, "Compatibility (and thus portability) is one of the greatest stumbling blocks to the development of successful load-sharing networks." In a recently reported survey of FORTRAN implementations, White and Ripley noted that only 60 percent of the implementations supported full ANSI FORTRAN 66 while 80 percent contained at most one restriction to the standard. However, all dialects surveyed contained non-ANSI extensions, and more than 90 percent of those were major extensions that could lead to extensive problems with portability (White and Ripley, 1977). A similar survey of BASIC implementations noted that while "the current versions satisfy the proposed ANSI standard for minimal

BASIC" most versions support considerable extensions of a wide variety resulting in "substantial differences between versions" (Lientz, 1976). I suspect that a similar situation exists with other widely used languages. Kenneth Bowles (1977) has observed:

> The manufacturers have persisted in extending the languages in proprietary ways in an effort to improve their competitive sales advantages. The result is that moving applications software from one machine to another is generally an expensive proposition, so expensive that end-users frequently prefer to re-program an application from the beginning.

In a university environment, portability is not only desirable, it is a way of life.

Institutional Change

A move to distributed systems may force a thorough airing of pricing algorithms and a change in institutional funding patterns for computing. For example, prime candidates for distribution are the many users with modest computing requirements, e.g., undergraduate students. Their needs can be met, to a large extent, by relatively small mini and micro systems now available. However, under some pricing algorithms, a shift of student computing use to minicomputers may force larger resources users of central systems to pay costs more closely approximating their true utilization of resources.

With tongue in cheek, distributed computing may offer an out for those who in the early 1970s installed illicit minis counter to existing institutional policy. By linking them together, distributed computing can be presented to the administration as a fait accompli.

Finally, when any institutional computing alternative is considered, the quality of the facility and services to be offered must be reviewed. While noting that different users require different qualities, Charles Mosmann (1976) makes an excellent analogy between the computing utility and the community water utility:

> Many communities are provided with water which is, although quite healthy, unpleasant to taste. Families in these communities tend to drink less water. Children do not complain about the quality of the water; they just drink less of it than they should. People wash with it and water their lawns, but they do not drink it. They drink something else, or nothing at all. There is nothing wrong with the water; it is just of a quality inappropriate for this purpose.

As with most computing alternatives, the advantages and disadvantages of distributed computing can be summarized as a mixed bag at best. The advantages may outweigh the disadvantages at one institution and the converse may be true at another. Some of the disadvantages may be overcome given the right set of circumstances. For example, I operate a center with stand-alone capability and considerable additional reliance on two systems 160 miles away. The problems of geographic distance noted earlier are very real. However, they can be worked out to a considerable degree. It is not easy, but it can be done.

The issue of selection and evaluation of computing alternatives boils down to how the institution really makes decisions about all matters of a pressing nature. Most computer alternatives are proposed couched in technological terms and jargon. However, the decision will be based less upon the technology than upon the particular institutional dynamics in effect at that time. These elements may or may not have anything to do with computing (Skelton, 1973). Distributed computing may succeed as a natural outgrowth of today's networks. Given the direction of technology, this certainly seems to be a logical extension. However, my feeling is that the true computational and quality needs of the users must be determined first, and then the system designed to meet those needs. If administrators in colleges and universities seek to employ the latest technology as an end unto itself, distributed computing will fail. Distributed technology will be employed on many campuses naturally. It will fail, however, because users will use less of it than they should. There is nothing intrinsically wrong with distributed computing, but the quality may be inappropriate for the uses.

References

Bowles, K. L., 1977. "An Appeal for Support of Manufacturer Independent Software," University of California, San Diego (March).

Chambers, J. A., and Poore, R. V., 1975. "Computer Networks in Higher Education: Socio-Economic-Political Factors," *Communications of the ACM* (April).

Down, P. J., and Taylor, F. E., 1976. *Why Distributed Computing?* London: National Computing Centre Publications.

Lientz, B. P., 1976. "A Comparative Evaluation of Versions of BASIC." *Communications of the ACM* (April).

Mosmann, C., 1976. "Evaluating Instructional Computing." University of California, Irvine.

Skelton, J. E., 1973. "The Games Universities Play." *Facts and Futures,* EDUCOM.

White, J. W., and Ripley, G. D., 1977. "How Portable are Mini-Computer FORTRAN Programs?" *Datamation* (July).

Wiseman, T., 1977. "Distributed DP Seen Efficient Business Tactic." *Computerworld,* September 26.

DISTRIBUTED ADMINISTRATIVE COMPUTING

9

Distributed Administrative Computing: Technical Issues

Fred H. Harris

Introduction

The theme of the 1977 EDUCOM Conference, "Closing the Gap Between Technology and Application," is a timely one. In numerous periodicals one can find an article or multi-page advertisement about new developments in computer technology and the new ways in which computing capability is being deployed. Computer center directors have also noticed a growing wave of salespeople talking to faculty and administrators on campus. If they are not already involved with the impact and application of new developments in the computer field, they soon will be.

Yet distributed data processing means various things to different people. For my purposes I think of it as a combination of distributed processing, distributed data, and distributed operational responsibility. In this definition distributed means spread among physically, geographically, and/or organizationally separate units. A number of perspectives or dimensions are important to distributed data processing. To identify major technical issues, the following are significant:

- environment
- function

- equipment
- software
- "network" organization
- support services
- quality factors

Environment is an important dimension because technical issues—or perhaps in this sense, technical choices and opportunities—cannot be divorced from their context. Indeed, the nature of the organization in which data processing is evolving into distributed data processing may well dictate which technical matters are issues and which are not. Only some aspects of the environment have technical impact on a distributed system. For example, the environment will certainly dictate the choice of network organization, ring versus hierarchical, or the need for both. The environment also sets the stage for the way in which function should be dispersed and the extent to which there are significant opportunities for replication of applications as well as function. Specific aspects of the environment that do influence technical development of a distributed system are:

- single campus versus multicampus
- centralized versus decentralized
- centrifugal versus centripetal
- structured versus unstructured

Technical Issues

On a case-by-case basis, distributed data processing must provide a range of functions and extend them ever closer to the end user:

- data entry
- transaction processing
- query
- database/file maintenance
- message switching

- electronic mail
- text processing
- graphics
- interactive
- batch
- online

The reader will observe in this list both traditionally recognized activities and others that are only now emerging. For a given administrative office or unit, the subset of functions required has significant impact on systems organization including both hardware and software.

In designing hierarchical distributed systems, the manager should spread the functions up and down the hierarchy by locating them where they can be performed with the best cost-performance ratio. Another rule of thumb is to place functions where both operational and systems aspects can be most effectively managed.

An important issue is the extent to which flexibility of choice in placement will exist. Choices will be made differently for different branches of the net.

Distributed data processing systems must include and support a range of equipment:

- data entry
- remote batch
- intelligent terminals
- minicomputers
- communication systems
- general purpose computers
- specialized input/output devices

Indeed, the exploding number of hardware options, and their rapidly decreasing costs, have introduced distributed data processing to the academic scene. However, communication systems and specialized input/output devices on my list are also important. The latter is often overlooked. Nevertheless, I see no major issues here. I think that computing managers in higher education institutions are in a relatively good position with hardware as compared to software and data.

Similarly, there are few surprises in the dimension of software:

- data entry
- database
- query languages
- report writers
- text editors
- applications-oriented languages
- general-purpose languages
- communication protocols
- process control languages
- security protocols

One component that is rarely stated explicitly as a requirement should be stressed—namely, process control languages or protocols. There is inherent in computing or data processing—in all layers of the organizational onion—the need for work or process management, scheduling, control, and so on. Historically, this need has been reflected in the evolution of the internal architecture of hardware and operating system, I/O subsystems and their interactions with main processors. Yet, an important layer has been largely ignored, the external one in batch systems which is usually handled manually. This layer consists of separate but interdependent files and/or jobs in both logical and temporal contexts. As files or data bases and processing are distributed, interdependencies will necessarily become more complex and will have to be managed through automated means. Software support for this purpose must be incorporated in a distributed system.

Another issue is software system or subsystem compatibility. As previously stated, computer center management is in relatively good shape with respect to hardware compatibility. RS 232s and plug-to-plug compatible devices are examples of that compatibility. However, few computing managers expect software compatibility to be achieved in the near future.

Another important dimension is data management and security. While the necessary solutions to data management and security problems are approaching in the centralized context, complexity will abound with dispersion, e.g., replication, aggregation, disaggregation, and concurrency.

Consider now several aspects of the dimension of "network" organization:

- centralized
- decentralized
- horizontal
- hierarchical
- partitioned
- replicated
- dynamic
- static
- internal
- external

Network is within quotation marks as a reminder that, as the list implies, one can think of a network in the asymptotic cases of centralized or decentralized systems without electronic communication connections. Moreover, we certainly think of networks in the senses of (1) hardware, data, and connectivity, (2) different levels of the corporate organization, and (3) time. These different senses each bear a special relationship to some aspects of "network" organization. Those relationships are illustrated as follows:

centralized decentralized	→	traditional unconnected "networks"

horizontal or ring hierarchical	→	primary choices of connected networks
partitioned replicated	→	data bases and applications
dynamic static	→	temporal
internal external	→	within a campus versus outside the campus

Here the overriding technical issues are upgradability and network standards including hardware components, protocols of various types, dictionaries, and so forth. No matter what the application or expected load or environment, initial requirements and solutions that meet them will both change. We must improve our ability to respond to such change in nondisruptive manners.

A dimension of importance to traditional computer center personnel and to administrative user groups as they consider the shift to distributed processing is that of support services. Aspects of this dimension are:

- management
- advice, consultation, review and training
- applications development and maintenance
- network and data control
- equipment operations and maintenance
- "value-added" specialized services

Again, there are both traditional and new types of the support services dimension on my list. The traditional ones will obviously change focus in a distributed system and some (for example, data entry personnel) may disappear altogether from the computer center's domain. But they will be replaced with even more demanding responsibilities for support in the areas of technical advice, control, and value-added services.

I wish to emphasize the central importance of network and data control as both a service and responsibility of the data processing group. If distributed data processing is to approach its potential, central planning and control is a must.

Finally, several factors influence quality as seen by the user:

- functional fidelity
- acceptable price
- appropriate performance
- ease of use
- reliability
- availability
- maintainability
- upgradability
- security

Functional fidelity means simply meeting user specifications, and not providing services in excess of user specifications. Since one's estimate of "too much" service will change over time, computing management must constantly be prepared to upgrade services.

These factors are most often compressed by users into a shorter list that includes cost, control, responsiveness, and security. In particular, responsiveness covers most quality factors in the longer list, whether one is discussing delays in response to an interactive query to a centralized database or to a request for a cosmetic maintenance change in an application program.

Summary

In summary, the major technical issues as I perceive them are:

- flexibility in placement of function
- process control
- software subsystem compatibility
- data management and security
- network standards
- upgradability

Inherent in these is the management of change!

10

Distributed Administrative Computing: Administrative Issues

J. C. Morrow

Introduction

Administrative issues arising in the application of distributed computing in university environments are conveniently grouped under four headings: planning, organizational changes, funding, and implementation of plans. In the following discussion, some specific applications of minicomputers in administrative offices are briefly described in order to illustrate the issues and related principles.

Planning

The discussion of planning is limited to only two of the many aspects of planning that deserve attention. The first is determination of the proper locus of institutional planning involving, or possibly involving, minicomputers. Should such planning originate in the administrative user units or in the data processing center? Per se, the origin of plans for minicomputer use should not be of great moment to anyone in an institution if the elaboration of the planning process takes the proper course. If the planning schedule allows sufficient time for the users to make an adequate analysis of the field of application, if the process allows the technical opinions of experts in computer technology to influence the selection of equipment, if it permits the director of the data processing center to present an opinion based on study of the impact of the proposed changes on the center and its users, if it includes examination by administrative officials who have general budgetary responsibility for the user unit and the data processing center, then the point of origin of the plan assumes a secondary importance.

Adequate review of proposals for new computer installations does more than just keep the various segments of the university informed. To leave planning for computer acquisition entirely to the individual user is to invite a kind of simple competition that can lead to great wastes of time and money. Administrators who seek to use computing equipment are not likely to be experts in computer technology, and they may blunder badly in making technical choices. In contrast, the computer center director in whose hands all computer planning is centralized may produce plans that are exemplary in their technical aspects but are insufficiently responsive to user need. In attempting to avoid these difficulties the institution need not deny itself the administrative advantage of charging a single individual with oversight of the development of a particular computer plan. The institution need only require that the several necessary consultations occur before the plan is approved.

At the University of North Carolina at Chapel Hill, the heads of user units and the head of the administrative data processing center alike are free to bring forward proposals for minicomputer acquisition. Any such plan must eventually reach the provost, who utilizes a computer advisory committee to conduct a review. The committee is quite heterogeneous with respect to the training, experience, type of responsibility, and academic interest of its members. The proposer of any computer acquisition, mini or otherwise, must convince the committee that the appropriate consultations have occurred and that the general plan of use is sound. The committee does not distribute money or pass judgment on budget availability; resource allocations are made by administrative officers of the university.

As a result of the activity of the computer advisory committee, anyone hoping to get a minicomputer has at least one firm encounter with persons who know hardware and the hardware market, who know both the strengths and the limitations of minicomputers, who know how to distinguish between computer problems and management problems, and who are not sales representatives. Persons seeking to acquire minicomputers for use in scientific research usually know the hardware field better than do those who would like to buy minicomputers for administrative offices. The advisory committee can help administrators avoid some impressive pitfalls. It is a commonplace that the mere existence of a good review committee brings out the best in the proposers of plans. Contact between the would-be minicomputer user and the director of central data processing before the fact of purchase greatly benefits both. The director cannot give the campus proper support without participating in the planning for administrative minicomputer use outside the data processing center.

The unevenness that characterizes plans arising in an institution which encourages the user units to take the planning initiative is ameliorated by a good review process. Some decentralization of planning seems to be particularly appropriate for the acquisition of minicomputers, since their relatively low cost tends to move the financial go/no-go decision close to the user and correspondingly far from the central university administration.

The second aspect of planning that needs attention is the sequence of steps in the planning process. It is essential that minicomputers, if deemed appropriate for a given situation, be adapted to serve administrative needs and not the other way around. The person who assumes that minis can solve all administrative problems is sure to compound some disasters. One must resist the impulse toward minis until one has clear evidence first that computing or more of it is the answer, and second that a minicomputer is the kind of computational equipment needed for the task.

The University of New Mexico's 1976 decision to install

four minicomputer systems (one in admissions, one in the cashier's office, one in registration, and one in its existing data processing center) was taken only after two important planning periods were completed. (Details of the use of minicomputers at the University of New Mexico have been reported by K. Harward, R. Legoza, D. Leurig, B. Leurig, F. Chreist, and L. J. Poulsen, "Maximizing Minis for a More Meticulous Method of Monitoring Multitudes," *College and University,* Summer 1977, pp. 414–417.) The first was devoted to a careful setting of goals for operations in the area of admissions and registration. After it became clear that reaching these goals would require additional computing power, the university used a second planning period to examine various options of new computer equipment. Only then did it decide to acquire four minicomputers rather than a large machine. The 70-percent growth in enrollment at New Mexico from 1965 to 1977 made progressively more arduous the 1965-style manual registration procedures, even though the institution periodically alleviated the pressure by making changes in the organization of its manual registration operation. The university's administrators decided to provide new kinds of registration services to students rather than just to cope with registration problems directly related to the increase in the size of its student body. In other words, the 1976 decision was to go beyond merely automating the existing manual operation. Specifically, administrators wanted, among other things, (1) to give the student freedom to select a course pattern and a section schedule limited only by overall degree requirements and the availability of places in sections; (2) to keep current and to display on a continuous basis the availability of places in all courses and sections of multisection courses; (3) to perform registration with the student present and to deliver to the student a hard copy of the entire schedule each time a change is completed; and (4) to enable the student to make as many changes as needed within the limits of the academic policies of the institution. Only after setting these major new goals and deciding to add computing power to the campus did the university administration compare the merits of using part of a large time sharing system to those of several minicomputers.

At the University of North Carolina at Chapel Hill, application of the principle that administrative plans should be put in order before computers are ordered has delayed for a while the consideration of the use of minicomputers in registration and admissions. Administrative plans are not yet in order because final development is not complete for an extensive, highly interlocked group of administrative information systems based on student data and, naturally enough, deeply dependent on information gathered by and held in the office of records and registration. This student information system ties together smaller systems in undergraduate admissions, graduate admissions, housing, student aid, records, registration, and the office of the cashier. Through the cashier system, the information system is linked with the university's main accounting system. Eighteen months ago, when the advantages of the student information system became clear, some potential users pressed for the immediate acquisition of small computing machines to speed up the realization of the benefits of the new system. They were diplomatically rebuffed by both the supervisors of the administrative units and the software experts in central data processing. The team of managers and systems analysts responsible for designing the plan declined to make any specific recommendation favoring either the addition of minicomputers or expansion of central data processing, since the design was incomplete. The proper time for moving on to hardware considerations is, however, quite near, and the experience of other universities with minicomputers in registration offices will be taken into account when the decisions are made.

Even though it may seem obvious that close analysis of the administrative aspects of programs and the setting of administrative goals should precede the planning stage devoted to decisions between central and distributed computing, experience shows that harping on this point unfortunately still is necessary.

One must find the middle ground between succumbing to minicomputer sales pressure and rejecting minicomputers because they are so fashionable. Insistence on thorough analysis of the user's administrative needs prior to the selection of equipment strengthens the quality of planning.

Organizational Changes

Administrators must be prepared to deal with a variety of personnel problems resulting from the impact on their staffs of computer acquisition. Employees may greatly fear minicomputers, because their arrival can lead directly to work force reductions, and falling minicomputer prices reinforce these fears. The threat is probably greater to temporary staff than it is to full-time staff, since employers usually feel more strongly committed to the latter. Introduction of the registration minicomputer at the University of New Mexico made possible the reduction of temporary staff from 200 to 21.

Reduction of the size of the work force need not have a uniformly bad impact on morale among employees. Some find in the changed situation an opportunity to pick up new skills through use of computing equipment and, as a result, to improve their status. Some who are displaced by machines find that release from drudgery now relegated to minicomputers permits their reassignment to interesting tasks. If client dissatisfaction is sharply reduced by the installation of minicomputers (if, for example, long lines and frustrating delays disappear), the staff will doubtless find daily contact with the public much pleasanter than before.

Among problems noted by a personnel supervisor to be caused by a newly arrived minicomputer may be the adjustment of job descriptions and attempted reclassification of employees who now operate the computer. Personnel departments typically do not make these changes easily or rapidly, and reclassifications may have to be accompanied by salary increases. The supervisor who has to find these new funds will not necessarily be reclassified upward or raised in salary. Also, the supervisor may eventually feel uneasily dependent on or even threatened by the growing power of subordinates who "know the machine."

The new operations made possible by the introduction of a minicomputer may require the head of a unit to create new administrative links between the unit and the consumers of its services. For example, the physical plant department at the University of North Carolina at Chapel Hill has had to organize a liaison committee of university building inhabitants and physical plant personnel to deal with problems surrounding the arrival of a minicomputer at the heart of a building temperature and humidity control system. A prerequisite to the successful shift from manual to real-time computer-controlled adjustments of valves and vents is the determination of conditions needed in each separate space of each building. The humidity and temperature needed for the proper functioning of laboratory equipment or for the survival of experimental animals must be known before the system is turned over to a computer. The impact of computer malfunction must be predicted, and arrangements for regular review of operating conditions must be made. Creation of a group such as that described above often improves the level of understanding between faculty and physical plant staff. Academicians and physical plant personnel rarely have the kinds of day-to-day contacts that make each well acquainted with the concerns of the other.

The attractive pricing and technical power of small machines has lent credence to the idea that complete decentralization of computing is inevitable. I do not believe this is so. In many settings an administrative data processing center with a large computer still provides the most efficient means of performing certain computing tasks and justifies the maintenance of a sizable pool of highly trained computer personnel. The user for whom a minicomputer is purchased may be heavily dependent on the technical personnel in the data processing center to show the staff how to use its new equipment. These training needs can be pressing at times well after the period of initial installation, for universities often have high rates of turnover among personnel in administrative offices. The success of minicomputers in initial applications encourages the use of the equipment in solving more complicated problems, and additional staff training at the programming level, if not the operating level, often proves to be necessary. Most of the burden of this retraining falls on the staff of the data processing center.

Minicomputers, rather than replacing computers in centers, tend to support centers by bringing out the best in large CPUs. Moving data cleanup from a central machine to small machines in users' offices improves the quality of data eventually transmitted to the center, concentrates the use of the large machine on tasks for which its design and capacity give maximum efficiency, and gives the user staff better control over the information going into the central machine and into the central files. These advantages have been realized in recent installations of intelligent terminals in the cashier's office and the business offices of the medical center's private patient service at the University of North Carolina at Chapel Hill. Keystroking and validation are now carried out on the terminals in these offices and certain operations are then performed by the minicomputers. The results are transmitted to central data processing. The use of cassette tapes permits an operator to schedule keystroking at any time, even when the central data processing machine is inaccessible or down. Morale of the clerical staff has risen because the entire computer system now appears always to be waiting for the operator; formerly the reverse seemed to be true. The difficult computing tasks and complex file maintenance operations are still carried out by the central machine and its staff. Since no major new responsibilities have been assumed by the cashier and the private patient service, the distribution of computing power has provided net relief, but the staff and equipment in the data processing center are as important as distributed data processing in achieving that desirable result.

The prospects for successful decentralization of computing depend in many instances on the centralization of control of standards and data definitions. The imposition of control may not be welcome at the outset, but it is much preferred over computational chaos. Central control of standards does not imply centralization of all things administrative. Consider, for example, the results of minicomputer installation on the Dearborn campus of the University of Michigan. Equipment was needed to help gather and transmit administrative data to Ann Arbor. The charges for telephone lines were sufficiently great to rule out Dearborn's online use of the computer in the data processing center at Ann Arbor. Setting up in Dearborn a center self-sufficient in staff and equipment was judged to be unnecessarily duplicative and expensive. Both people and machines would have been repeating what was already being done well on the larger campus. The minicomputer equipment obtained for Dearborn acts as an intelligent terminal, which, after cleaning the input data, serves as a remote job entry device with immediate feedback to verify the accuracy of transmission. The option of activating either the Dearborn or the Ann Arbor printer for output is very convenient. Of special interest for the present discussion is the point that adding the minicomputer permitted certain administrative operations to be decentralized. Space utilization studies, maintenance of equipment inventories, and some similar tasks can now be performed by the staff at Dearborn. The resulting information is understandably valuable to the Dearborn administration. The Ann Arbor Internal Audit Department has retained strict control of standards for moving data from the smaller to the larger machine. To this insistence on compatibility may be attributed in no small measure the success of the administrative decentralization based on operation of the minicomputer installation.

Funding

Computing problems may have multiple solutions, and the selection of one over the others often is based on cost alone. For this reason it is essential that the purchaser attempt to calculate all of the costs and to look beyond the initial cost to the eventual outlay. The person who wants to buy a minicomputer must take into account personnel costs as well as machine prices. Creating a staff which is deep in technical expertise can be expensive. The purchaser must look at all the equipment costs, not just that of the CPU. Hanging lots of peripherals on a mini can be costly. Sharing a large machine with many other users may have its drawbacks, but sharing the cost of upgrading the equipment of an administrative data processing center is more attractive than going it alone. The burden of upgrading a mini usually falls on the budget of a single user. Moreover, budget officers may not embrace a plan to discard a saturated mini and purchase another one but instead may ask one to live with the original purchase.

The decision to favor the purchase of four minicomputers in the administrative offices of the University of New Mexico and to forego in 1976 the acquisition of major new time sharing equipment was based mainly on the lower cost of the minis. The time sharing equipment, though more desirable technically, was also more expensive. The cost and availability of software were considerations in the comparison.

Administrators at the University of North Carolina at Chapel Hill recently made a careful study of the computing needs of the student stores. The goal of the study was to extend the computerization of the student stores' operations. This unit has for some time had its textbook ordering and accounts receivable work done in the administrative data processing center. With the aid of the center, student stores compared the service that might be had through expansion of the center's machine and the service that might be rendered by a captive minicomputer. A primary advantage of the mini was that it would free student stores from the inconvenience of the center's tight scheduling. A second advantage was that student stores, through purchase of a mini, could proceed to add computing power immediately and would not have to wait until the center could effect expansion. Peculiarities of funding are responsible for the second advantage. Student stores operates entirely on receipts, and shifts in budget are made rather quickly if the necessary receipts are at hand. The administrative data processing center, however, gets major support from state appropriations and from grant and contract overhead funds. Changes in the center's budget require substantial amounts of time, and they may not be made without obtaining the approval of a number of boards and commissions.

The absence of a programming staff in student stores was a deterrent to the acquisition of a minicomputer. Importation of a successful software package developed by Brigham Young University for its stores would have offset this disadvantage somewhat, but adaptation of the software would still have required the attention of skilled programmers. The need for compatibility with the center's large machine restricted the field of appropriate small machines. Nonetheless, the center staff joined staff of the student stores to recommend acquiring a minicomputer rather than waiting for the center to find ways to expand its facilities. The recommendation proved to be unacceptable because of high cost. The cost increases which would come from adding programming staff for student stores were not looked upon with favor. Furthermore, concentrating the burden of funding on the student stores' budget would mean a noticeable cut in the short run in the student stores' annual surplus, which is exclusively devoted to scholarships. The administration decided to wait for the center expansion, in order to save money in the salary lines and to protect scholarship support from a temporary setback.

In the past, centralization of computing has been sold on the basis of its cost advantages. Future decentralization will have to be sold on the same basis. One must not forget that decentralization results in the distribution of budgetary responsibility for computing. Small administrative units that traditionally had little or no money for equipment may have trouble getting the new funds for buying a minicomputer. New budgets for small machines may be hard to get from administrators who have formed the habit of defending the budget of a large computing center. Before seeking new funds or partitioning the budget of a central computing facility in order to buy administrative minicomputers, administrators will look for unused capacity wherever it can be found. In the school of medicine at Chapel Hill, for example, the administration found that a small machine acquired for research had unused capacity, and it quickly put on the machine programs to keep track of its salary budget, space utilization records, and grant proposal status. Thus, the time of even small machines may have to be divided between scientific and administrative applications. The management problems which attend the use of a single computer by scientists and administrators may be just as pressing in the case of the minicomputer as in the case of equipment in a large data processing center.

Implementation of Plans

The compactness of minicomputers does not guarantee that they will take root and flourish the instant they are wheeled onto the floor of an administrative office. Some provision of time and money must generally be made for parallel operation of the old and new methods of data handling. An accurate calculation of costs always should include evaluation of the cost of duplicate processing during the initial period of use. If a complex arrangement of minis is to be set up, one should not expect all offices necessarily to reach proficiency in computer use at the same time. Plans that require this simultaneity should be viewed with some suspicion. No arrangements should be regarded so highly as to be exempted from regular review. It is safe to say that, in this regard, distributed administrative computing is no different from any other kind of computing.

11

Distributed Administrative Computing: Reaction and Overview

Laurence H. Baker

Introduction

When we consider what is conceptually possible with today's technology, it is easy to conceive of exciting new administrative systems that will revolutionize current modes of operation (Harris, p. 103). However, when administrative issues (Morrow, p. 111) are considered, excitement about what is possible should be tempered with the reality that innovation and change may be a threat to those who must use what results from new administrative systems.

In short, technical and management issues interact to influence

- how and when new technology should be employed,
- what is practical in a specific environment,
- system integration versus specialization, and
- the appropriate approach to planning administrative systems.

How and When New Technology Should Be Employed

The number of alternative solutions to administrative system problems is large. Today's technology suggests

- low-cost hardware,
- low-cost, reliable data communications facilities,
- easy to use, flexible systems software capabilities, and
- interactive systems which can be used to support new administrative systems produced with increased programmer productivity.

However, these capabilities do not result in immediate implementation of new systems that satisfy everyone's perceived requirements.

The user environment must be considered. Its dimensions in higher education often include students, faculty, administrators and staff, the existing administrative system environment, and the interdependence of administrative system functions. New systems and procedures cannot be designed and successfully implemented without consideration of these dimensions.

Factors that influence the user environment must also be considered. They include education about computing for administration, vendor promotion, the decision process involved with any change, and the role of the existing computer center staff.

Successful use of new technology in implementing new administrative systems depends on

- the user community understanding the technology,
- the extent to which administrators understand how to manage it using new procedures,
- the extent to which it satisfies all requirements,
- the extent to which conversion problems from the old to new systems are analyzed and considered, and
- how well those involved in the decisions required understand the benefits of change.

What Is Practical in a Specific Environment?

To determine what form of a distributed computing system can be implemented best, one must consider the elements of a specific environment for administrative systems:

- Organizational relationships versus functions to be supported
- Levels within an organization
- Technical support available
- Management experience with technology
- User experience with technology
- Acquisition policy regarding new resources required
- Existing computing and data communications environment

The existing stage of administrative systems development and its implementation can influence how rapidly revolutionary changes can be made. Several questions should be considered in assessing what is practical in a specific environment. (1) Are present systems stabilized and well documented so they do not require ongoing technical support? (2) Can specialized systems serving independent organizational units be integrated to eliminate redundant collection and maintenance of common data elements? (3) What issues of privacy and security must be considered relative to data elements not required by all organizational units requiring access to an integrated data base? (4) Is management willing to make the decisions required to support changing data collection, entry and processing requirements? (5) Have criteria and evidence been developed which support implementing a new system using new technology? (6) What steps need to be taken to show management and users how to manage and utilize new technology? (7) Have communications procedures to provide user support to all levels in an organization been established? (8) To what extent have data element definitions been standardized across organizational units?

System Integration versus Specialization

Most early approaches to the development of administrative systems resulted in the design of a system to support each functional requirement, e.g., payroll, personnel, admissions, student records, financial aid billing, faculty workload analysis, space utilization analysis, receivables, and payables. The advantages of this approach include: elimination of organizational problems and avoidance of some issues associated with privacy, security, and data base ownership. The approach also simplifies design requirements and often reduces system resources needed. In addition it reduces development and implementation time, and provides greater direct control of data processing to the users.

Several disadvantages also result from designing separate systems for all administrative applications. Data collection efforts are often redundant, and data elements are drawn from different sources in files supporting different organizational units. Because the integrated system is so complex, the final system often suffers from poor system design, shorter system life, and poor documentation. Increased conversion effort is required when hardware systems must be replaced. Finally, because nonstandard data elements are used, special processing is required to merge data from different systems.

The separate system approach is still promoted by organizational units and vendors who minimize the importance of technical support requirements. However, this very argument tends to magnify the disadvantages listed above.

System integration can be realized where the functional requirements of each organizational unit are defined and a system is designed that results in

- standard data element definitions,
- one-time collection of each data element,
- initial processing closest to the point of origin,
- location of data elements in data bases where they are required, and
- use of consolidated data bases where data elements should be integrated across organizational units.

A successful integrated system can only occur where requirements of different organizational units can be coordinated, special technical assistance provided, and standards developed, and where users and technical support personnel work together to prepare a system definition and implementation plan. The advantages of system integration include

- elimination of redundant data collection efforts,
- elimination of common data elements from different sources in different files and reports,
- good system design,
- longer system life,
- good documentation,
- minimization of conversion efforts where hardware systems must be replaced,
- standard data elements,
- elimination of special processing required to manage data from different systems,
- cooperation among organizational units in development of a shared data base, resulting in better response to management requirements,
- utilization of large computers where required and handling of local tasks with terminals or minicomputers,
- realization of cost savings through acquisition of common software and hardware,
- development of common application software, and
- sharing of common software using common hardware.

Planning Administrative Systems

The appropriate approach toward planning administrative systems is a function of

- organizational complexity at many functions and levels,
- status of administrative systems,
- status of computing resources,
- level of understanding of technology by management,
- locus of support for planning, and
- policy toward acquisition of computing resources.

Should the initiative for planning be left to users? Should management establish a unit to take the initiative in planning? The answer to these questions will vary with each organization. However, as the size and complexity of an organization increases, the benefits to be gained from establishing a unit to take the initiative in planning can be great. Some of them follow:

- Sharing software and hardware
- Discounts on resource acquisitions
- System integration
- Development of standards
- Longer system life
- Few unique systems
- Economies of specialization used when appropriate
- Economies of scale used as required
- Minimal and efficient use of data communication

The Future

The issues outlined are not simple, but the tools available are more powerful than ever before. What is possible is limited only by our ability to define requirements and design systems to provide the maximum benefits to our users. However, if these tools are to benefit administrative users, those administrators must understand them, see opportunities for improvement, and not be threatened by their use.

INSTRUCTIONAL SYSTEMS

12

Instructional Systems: Technical Issues

Alfred Bork

Today's Situation

Everyone knows that instruction is one of the major roles of colleges and universities. College and university requests for funds from legislatures and from the public are usually justified on those grounds. Universities also engage in other activities in addition to instruction, research, and public service, but instruction is the most visible part of their work and the part that public institutions are most likely to be funded for by their state legislatures. This discussion is concerned with the *instructional* uses of computers in colleges and universities in the broadest sense of the term.

The term "instructional use of computers" has quite different meanings to different individuals. It is convenient to divide the area into three aspects. The first concerns learning about computers: how to program them, how to construct them, or how to design the languages associated with them. The second concerns the use of the computer within a variety of different courses for problem solving activity. In the more advanced courses, problem solving often can lead to budding research activities. Third, the computer is a direct aid to students in learning, in a variety of subject areas.

Learning about Computers

Computers will be important to the student's major field of study, perhaps more generally important. One of the widest current applications of computers in higher education is teaching students to program and familiarizing them with computers. Introductions to the computer and its languages are typically offered in computer science courses. Computer appreciation courses fall in this category. Introductory, discipline-oriented programming courses are increasingly offered outside of computer science. Many students do not need to spend a full semester or full quarter learning to manipulate FORTRAN; they can learn enough in a much shorter time to work on problems specific to the discipline. Programming is also taught through service courses, typically organized by the computer center. These are usually noncredit courses, and are often briefer than those offered in academic departments.

In all three cases a number of issues appear. First, is the approach to be interactive or batch? In most facilities where interactive is possible, instructors prefer to use it. I regard most of the arguments for batch as "sour grapes" arguments, justifying what must be done, but little hard empirical evidence exists on this issue. The few attempts to obtain such evidence seem inadequate. The second issue is whether the student is to be taught graphic capabilities in the early stage, or whether programming is to proceed entirely in a nongraphic environment. Nongraphics accounts for perhaps 95 percent of current beginning programming courses, but there are some strong advantages in allowing even the beginning student to access graphic commands, and a number of recent innovative introductory programs have moved in that direction. Again, the question of resources becomes an issue; students can quickly use graphics only if computer resources and graphic displays are available.

In teaching programming to students, both the language and the method of teaching are important factors. Extensive discussions have dealt with which languages are "best" for introducing students to programming. Wildly different assertions are found in the literature, and some languages are advertised as being easier for the beginner to learn. My experience is that the rate for learning languages is almost the same for all languages.

A recent trend, particularly in computer science departments, is toward use of structured languages such as PASCAL. The term structured programming covers a variety of good programming practices. The empirical (as opposed to the anecdotal) evidence supporting structured programming is weaker than one would desire for such an important issue, but the direction is promising.

Almost all the major languages have their strong adherents. In many cases the instructor has no choice because only a single language is available. It is interesting to note that, even in those cases, the instructor often becomes an extremely strong supporter of that language!

The method by which programming is taught will be dependent on whether interactive or batch capabilities are available. Older courses, and some contemporary courses, took a grammatical approach, teaching the grammatical components of the language before letting students write programs. New methods often start with the "whole program" approach, showing the student full programs. Another approach, with an interactive language that will work in an immediate mode (producing results on single line inputs), involves letting the student type in items and watch what happens.

Another important aspect of learning about computers is computer appreciation. The student in such courses does not necessarily learn to program, although simple programming tasks may be included in the course. Rather, the attempt is to develop a student's conscious attitude about the computer and its roles, both good and bad, in our current and future society. Although these courses are much discussed, it is my impression that they are not offered to as many students as one is led to believe. It may be that there is not enough programming content left if one removes programming from such courses.

Finally, the category of learning about computers must

include all the nonintroductory courses typically offered by computer science departments, or by other departments that teach computer science. Most of the students in more advanced courses will be computer science majors or majors in the sciences with a minor in computer science. Discussions of typical computer science curricula, and comments on the types of courses offered, are beyond the scope of this paper. However, it should be noted that some of these courses are misleading to students. Students will often see themselves as preparing for a programming career, but more typically the courses are oriented toward graduate study in computer science. Perhaps a separate set of courses is needed for each of these functions. To some extent these separate courses do exist in other departments outside of computer science. For example, it is not uncommon for a graduate school of business to teach COBOL or other important business languages as part of its curriculum and to pursue this beyond the elementary programming stage.

Problem Solving in Courses

The second major instructional use of computers is as a problem-solving tool in courses. Although the sciences and engineering, particularly the physical sciences, represent the main focus, a wide variety of academic areas are involved.

Much of the teaching of programming within academic disciplines other than computer science is directed toward this purpose. The computer is to be a tool that the student can employ as an aid in learning the subject. It serves as an intelligence amplifier, increasing the student's capability to solve problems. Computer-based problems are often inaccessible without the computer, more complex, and therefore closer to those in the real world, than the problems in the same courses handled without computers. Sometimes faculty refer to this style of computer use as adjunctive.

Many of the materials available from CONDUIT fall into the adjunctive classification. CONDUIT, sponsored by the National Science Foundation, is centered at the University of

Iowa; its purpose is the propagation of computer-based teaching materials. From both a pedagogical and a transferability point of view, CONDUIT reviews computer-based learning materials and makes them widely available. About fifty modules are currently available through CONDUIT, with total sales of about 1,000 modules.

Problem-solving activities involving computers can occur at different levels within a course. They can be an addition to the existing course, a minor, perhaps optional, excursion; or they can be fundamental to the course, allowing new approaches not available without the computer as a problem-solving aid. This last possibility, although more exciting, is still relatively rare in higher education. A related activity is the construction and use of computer modules. These offer the student a range of experience that can lead to increased learning, and they can aid in building student intuition.

One major difficulty with using the computer to any wide extent as a problem and model solving aid within courses is that existing textbooks in almost all areas completely ignore the existence of the computer. Publishers have issued supplementary texts, but have remained otherwise unconvinced that they should be publishing computer-based teaching materials. Since most courses are dependent on a main text, the computer will not make a sizable impact as a problem-solving aid until such texts are available. If faculty cannot persuade existing commercial publishers to move in this direction, it may be necessary for the universities, or organizations like EDUCOM, to support the necessary publishing activity in order to realize the full potential of this use of the computer.

The Computer as a Direct Aid in Learning

The third and final use considered is use of the computer directly by students to help them to learn in an academic area. The computer here is a "teaching machine," but this phrase is too narrow and too misunderstood to cover the full range of possibilities. The computer can be used as a direct aid only in an interactive environment in which the student works with a time sharing terminal or a stand-alone computer. The term "mainline" is sometimes employed; in this situation the computer is functioning as a textbook, a lecturer, or a discussion section. The students, sitting at individual displays, are carrying on a "conversation" or dialog with the writer of the material through the medium of the computer. Often several students will participate, discussing the material together and so increasing the learning potential.

In the best such material, the student not only plays a very active role, but the entire process is also tailored to the individual student's abilities, understanding, and attitudes. Thus, the student is responding to questions, and, depending on the particular response, can move in different directions. Learning can become an active situation, with the student a constant participant, compared to a typical lecture situation in which the participation of many students consists of frantically writing everything down as fast as they can.

The computer dialog is relatively rare at present. If one were to go into institutions of higher education and classify educational computer use in the three categories suggested, probably no more than 5 percent would fall into the third category. I will argue later that computer dialogs will be the most rapidly growing area of instructional computing in universities. Eventually it will become the dominant area.

A number of projects at the university level have devoted considerable energy to exploring computer dialogs as a direct aid to learning. The most well known is PLATO, initially centering at the University of Illinois but now a commercial venture of Control Data Corporation. The TICCET project, from the Mitre Corporation and Brigham Young University, is a second well-known project. My own project, the Physics Computer Development Project at Irvine, has also done extensive work in this direction. All these projects have employed graphic capabilities; it seems extremely likely that instructional computing will be dominated by graphics in the future.

Several types of dialog usage are possible. Perhaps the most obvious is tutorial, in which the student gains an understanding similar to that which would be attained in a lecture but in a more active and individualized fashion. Another example is drill and practice, the constant generation of problems to aid student performance, with detailed diagnostic assistance. Games with educational value can serve for both motivational and learning purposes. Controllable worlds, in which students have access to facilities not typically available in the world, either through the calculational capabilities of the computer or through its large data storing possibilities, are other interesting and important examples. Assisting students with particularly difficult issues in courses, such as the solving of problems, is a promising category. Finally, the use of the computer to generate or administer tests and to offer precisely tailored help to students in trouble as soon as trouble occurs is another important area.

Current Hardware and Languages

One of the difficulties with widespread use of the computer in instructional environments is the range of computers and languages involved. There are, however, some "dominant" possibilities. It's no secret that IBM has made very large inroads in educational computing, just as it has in every other aspect of computing. A recent Datamation survey, considering all aspects of computing, shows IBM with half the market; this includes terminals, software services, and peripherals as well as the computers themselves. In the small time sharing systems PDP-11 systems are becoming the most common machines, and in the medium-scale time sharing system Digital Equipment Corporation is also an important educational factor, particularly with the DEC System 20.

A list of the major instructional computer systems on the nine University of California campuses illustrates the tremendous diversity of equipment available:

Campus	*Equipment*
Berkeley	Control Data 6400
	DEC PDP-11/70 (4)
	Nova ECLIPSE
Davis	Burroughs 6700
Irvine	DEC PDP-10
	Honeywell Sigma 7
	DEC PDP-11/45
Los Angeles	IBM 360/91
Riverside	IBM 360/50
Santa Barbara	IBM 360/75
	DEC PDP-11/45
Santa Cruz	IBM 360/40
	DEC PDP-11/45
San Diego	Burroughs 6700
San Francisco	IBM 370/45

Often instructional use of the computer is ignored in the process of choosing computers in universities. For example, research considerations may dominate because a particular group in a department has need for the extremely powerful computational capabilities in FORTRAN. Alternatively, a computer science department may dominate the selection process because of its strong needs for LISP. Since these and other interests are often politically very powerful in the choice of a computer, the choice is often not in the best interests of the majority of the campus.

There is a tremendous variation in computer languages as well as hardware and no sign of any change in the situation. Even the same language on different machines is usually not transferable. Because of its emphasis on transportability, CONDUIT tries to work in PFORT, a subset of FORTRAN developed by Bell Laboratories that is particularly portable. Because of the proliferation of computer languages, students can use computing more effectively if they learn several languages.

The Next Few Years for Instructional Systems

In this section I consider the likely developments which universities and colleges will confront in the next few years, particularly as they relate to computers. These issues impinge on more general aspects of university policy that are considered at the end of this section.

Period of Rapid Change

There is universal agreement that computer technology is in a period of extremely rapid evolution, and that no end to that evolution is in sight. For the next few years or for the longer range possibilities, all planning must be based on this expected rapid change.

Because of this rapid evolution, the raw cost of computing equipment power will continue to decline even more rapidly than in the past. Many of the technologies that were developed in the laboratory ten years ago, such as large-scale integration, are only now coming into commercially available systems. Soon it will be possible to put whole computers on chips. Memory, too, is becoming more compact and less expensive. Many figures are given to describe this evolution; one of the most common is that the cost of computing hardware is expected to go down by a factor of approximately ten in the next seven years. New systems will be cheaper than existing ones, and be more capable for both central machines and peripheral devices.

The significant decrease in hardware costs will not imply such dramatic decreases in total expenditures for computers. Other costs associated with computers, such as costs for administrative staff, will continue to rise. Further, instructors will demand increasingly sophisticated facilities; graphic capabilities, for example, will often be an addition to current capabilities. On balance, some decreases will occur for initial and maintenance costs as new generation equipment is purchased.

Another aspect of rapid evolution will be the rise in the importance of stand-alone or one-on-one computers. In this situation students will work with their own computers in an interactive environment. From the student point of view the interaction will not differ greatly from that in a time sharing system, but from an institutional point of view there will be great differences.

The stand-alone systems will be relatively inexpensive; currently sophisticated systems are available in the $5,000 to $15,000 range, and the increasingly available personal computers cost even less. The Commodore PET sells for $600. Costs will decline. Thus, a decision to buy a single unit will not involve the expenditure of money needed to buy a medium-scale time sharing system, and experimentation with the use of this equipment will not require the major institutional decisions involved in the past. However, as projects move from experimental to more general usage, many stand-alone units will be purchased, and expenditures will be nontrivial. Some control over the type of machine purchased may be necessary. Estimates based on current equipment indicate a hardware cost, for extensive usage in large class environments, of about $30 per student per year.

A device that works primarily in a stand-alone mode can occasionally access a large remote computer for special needs. Such access might provide electronic mail interchange and computer conferencing among students and between students and teachers. Large or rapidly changing data bases could continue to be accessed remotely. Massive computational needs might also be done on a large machine. In an interactive testing environment, a number of stand-alones might share a small central machine whose only function was record keeping. In all these cases the student might not know that another processor is involved. Large time sharing systems may also still be important in the development of educational materials.

Questions of organization with regard to stand-alones will also be important. These machines may be owned by individual departments, libraries, learning resource centers, or extension services rather than by the central computer facility. However, some central services, such as maintenance and programming services, will still be required. Some schools are beginning to move in this direction already, and the movement will be much greater during the next several years. Some of the organizational and management problems associated with stand-alone systems will need additional attention.

Another result of the rapid evolution of modern technology will be the increased availability of graphic capability to all students. The importance of visual information in an instructional environment can be vigorously argued. The fact that it has been so seldom used up to this time is a result of the evolution of computer systems. In the past, graphics appeared to be an expensive addition to computing capability. Now, however, graphics is only a minor cost increment, and it seems inconceivable that graphics will not be widely utilized with students.

How can the administrator and the faculty member react to rapid change? The key idea is flexibility. It will be impossible to make decisions that will last for twenty-five years or even two years. Plans developed each five years will be inadequate. A continual assessment within the institution will be required to determine how the institution can best respond to the situation. The assessment process must clearly involve a range of people including the faculty most interested in exploring the uses of the computer in instruction. Since these faculty will already have vested interests, a fair assessment will demand administrative skill.

Conventional computer centers will need to evolve to meet these new needs. Strong leadership in this area will be essential. Given the technical nature of this area, it is unlikely that many existing academic administrators can provide the leadership needed to maintain this flexibility, unless these administrators are both trained in instructional uses of computers and spend a major portion of their time on this activity. In an environment where choice of a major computer happens only once every seven or eight years, older administrative structures might have been usable. In an environment where choices will have to be made almost constantly, other structures will be essential. I expect many schools to ignore this warning, and I predict that the consequences will be unpleasant.

Increased Use of Dialog Material

Full potential of computer dialogs as an aid to student learning are just beginning to be realized, but the prospects are very exciting. We can look forward to an increase in the quality of education possible as the number of dialogs available increases very rapidly. The factors to be pointed out in the next section, concerning the beginning of commercial availability of such material, also will be important. The factors pointed out several years ago in the EDUCOM conference on factors inhibiting the use of computing in instruction are still present; the lack of suitable material is still a major barrier.

A major advantage of computer dialogs as a new learning medium will be that schools will be able to offer effective education to a wider range of students, including students from underprivileged backgrounds. Because of the flexibility and individualization of computer-based learning materials, students with less than adequate previous preparation can be aided directly. Learning resource centers and other similar organizations, will become increasingly important as sources of such aid. Graphic capabilities will be important because these "new" students are often less apt with purely verbal learning material.

Most schools are unable to cope at the present time with any large amount of usage of this type. Present computer capabilities are already overloaded, and are probably being used for these strictly instructional functions in a relatively small amount of the time. Hence additional time sharing or stand-alone capability will be the only way of meeting this demand. Schools can, of course, refuse to meet it, but then they will be increasingly cutting themselves off from an important learning device, and therefore increasingly shortchanging students, particularly the students mentioned in the previous paragraph.

Another type of problem will arise because of the very conservative nature of many university faculty and administrators.

Most faculty follow the teaching methods that they saw as undergraduates. Often they do not understand new learning techniques, and are unwilling to spend the time to investigate the possibilities. A faculty member interested in employing the computer in learning may have a difficult battle to fight with unsympathetic, or even hostile, administrators. My own experiences provide some interesting documentation of this point! Much better administrative understanding is required for computer dialog development in the next few years.

Commercial Availability of Dialog Material

Control Data Corporation has already begun to market computer-based learning material in the PLATO system. At least one other company, Educulture, is already working with authors to produce materials to be marketed on stand-alone machines.

These steps out of the cottage industry signal a major educational development. The authors of computer-based teaching materials have had to be hardy group, willing to perform many tasks not directly related to the development of such materials. Efficient and effective computer authoring systems will enable teachers to function primarily as *teachers,* leaving such tasks as coding, checking, marketing, and distribution to the commercial vendors. Authors will work in a way similar to that in which they currently prepare textbooks, and with similar incentives.

It is significant that both computer vendors and book publishers are interested in publishing dialogs. In neither case is the dialog a known product, so for both there is hesitation. However, as the large size of the potential market is understood, both these companies and new companies specifically developed for such purposes will come into existence. While few such new companies have been formed for higher education, one—the Computer Curriculum Corporation—is already playing a role in elementary and secondary education.

The services available for publishing dialogs will be like those available for books. The instructor will have easy access to material, and students will have easy ways of acquiring the material. Little action will be necessary on the part of universities, unless they decide they would like to become part of the commercial scene in this regard or unless they choose to regard the preparation of computer material as different from the preparation of texts. However, decisions will have to be made on purchasing both the hardware and the learning programs.

Computers and Nontraditional Modes of Education

Considerable change will occur in higher education in the immediate future. Some of these changes will be unrelated to computers, but all of them will interact with computer developments, and all are likely to lead to problems for traditional institutions.

One of the most exciting developments in education in recent years has been the Open University and its counterparts in this country, such as the University of Mid-America. As an educator I find these institutions offering an extremely interesting alternative to conventional education. While conventional institutions spend most of their instructional funds for classroom instruction, and almost none for course and curriculum development, the Open University reverses this trend completely. Several hundred thousand dollars may typically be spent by the Open University in developing a course, with great care given to the learning resources forming a part of that course. This material is utilized with students in ways that are much less costly, but—according to all current evidence—are just as effective or even more effective than traditional teaching methods.

Although the British Open University has made some use of computers, and is looking further into that possibility in some of its newer courses, this use has so far been minor. The fact that delivery systems for this material were quite expensive until recently has undoubtedly been a major factor. But decreasing costs and the existence of home computers will make the computer a continually more competitive learning mode for curriculum development in these institutions. Hence, the rise of computer use, and the rise of these new types of institutions, will support each other. Some movement toward greater use of computers for teaching is evident in recent data on the British Open University, as seen in Figure 1.

In recent years public libraries have been moving away from being mere purveyors of books toward providing a wider range of learning material for their clientele. The computer, particularly the stand-alone, will be a natural for that usage.

Finally, the beginning of home computer use, as already indicated, will affect the learning environment. The rise of the personal computer has been one of the most important recent changes in the computer field. Although many of the home computer machines are too simple and not reliable enough to support any extensive computer-based learning experience, that situation is changing rapidly. Vendors of learning material will see the home market as a profitable market, and more effective learning materials will soon be available for use in the home environment.

The Future

The trends just pointed out can be expected to extend into the future and to intensify. The development of stand-alone hardware will continue to move rapidly. More sophisticated systems, with considerably more computational power, more memory, and better peripheral devices will be available. Color graphics will soon be practical. The home videodisc system, made a part of the stand-alone educational computer system, will allow full multimedia capabilities as well as furnish an excellent marketing medium. Sound, for both input and output, is well within the range of current possibilities and could be expected soon in practical widely used systems. Better graphics, including full animation and drawings beyond simply line drawings, also are not far away for general student use.

Computer-based learning materials will be widely used because of the effectiveness of these materials and because of

HOW THE COMPUTER IS USED AS A TEACHING AID

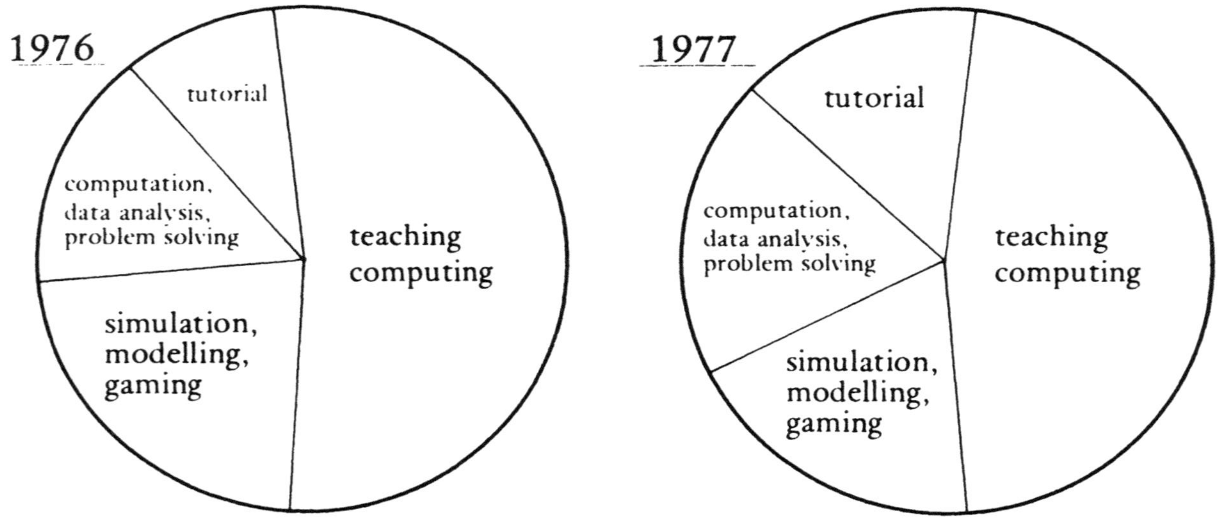

their increasing cost competitiveness with other learning modes. In its report, "The Fourth Revolution—Instructional Technology in Higher Education," the Carnegie Commission on Higher Education predicted that computer-based learning materials would be rapidly introduced in higher education during the period 1990 to 2000, and that from 2000 on, the materials would be in very widespread use. (The report suggests that materials would be developed in seven very large regional technology centers at government expense. Although such a system would have some interesting advantages, it does not seem likely at the present time.)

Today the Carnegie Commission's predictions seem conservative. I would move the dates ahead approximately five years. A major new factor, not anticipated in the Carnegie report, is the interest of commercial organizations in computer-based learning. Competition among vendors will undoubtedly be important. Furthermore, the expected development of home computers in the next few years, and the associated decline in computer prices generally because of mass production, will also speed the introduction of such material.

The period after 1980 will be one of considerable turmoil for education. Predictions indicate that the total number of students will decline during the 1980s, and that the universities will receive a smaller proportion of those students. As a result, universities will probably have more trouble raising funds, either through state legislatures or in other ways, than they do at the present time. Furthermore, no sign of change is apparent toward education in the present rather unfavorable political climate.

Because of these factors, the nontraditional modes of education are likely to receive increased attention and will move from little known institutions in this country to prominent institutions. In many cases, nontraditional programs and institutions will become competitors with the traditional universities, further cutting down university student populations.

Given these traumas for traditional higher education, how

will computers affect the situation? The effect can be positive or negative, depending on how institutions react. If universities choose to ignore the computer, and the nontraditional institutions (including public libraries) become stronger and more avid users of the computer as a learning mode, then traditional universities are likely to suffer. On the other hand, if universities use new computer developments to their best advantage, modifying their own internal structure to take advantage of the new technology, computer-based learning systems can become a positive asset in the difficult years ahead. Effective administrative leadership will be necessary to make the required changes in university structure. The issues are too complex to discuss fully here.

Finally, what about the faculty? The faculty is often worried about the effect that computers will have. They are typically a strong conservative force, resisting change. But for the faculty genuinely interested in student learning, there will be many benefits from using the computer as a learning device. Undoubtedly the faculty role will change when computers are widely employed. Lectures and group discussions will be of considerably less importance, except for a few highly charismatic lecturers. Routine activities such as record keeping will be left to the computer. Many faculty can be expected to spend a great deal more time working individually with students, particularly helping students with learning problems that the computer cannot solve. For many (but not all), this will seem to be a good bit more rewarding and exciting than lecturing to 500 students! Used properly, the computer can lead to a more humanistic approach to education.

13

Instructional Systems: Administrative Issues

Joseph Lipson

Introduction

There are so many administrative issues connected with the university that they constitute a fertile field for creative incompetence. When administrators cannot do the job they were hired to do, they can easily select something else to do that is more enjoyable. Hardly anyone notices.

Administrators are primarily decision makers, even though their decisions are constrained by various forces and dictated by political considerations. Whether by consensus, leadership, or some other process, administrators are the formal decision makers. They set policy, set priorities, allocate resources, and delegate authority. They establish procedures that can facilitate, slow, or block certain events (such as ordering minicomputers that might compete with the central campus facility). They commission both internal and external studies that result in recommendations that may determine the course of computing and instructional computing for many years to come.

Some administrative questions are specifically related to instructional systems using computers. How are decisions made to purchase computers or computing services? How is the vendor selected? How is the decision to purchase or lease made? How is the hardware configuration determined? How will the isolation of administrative, research, and instructional computing be effected? What will be the balance between centralized, decentralized, and autonomous acquisition decisions? How are various aspects of computing budgeted? How frequently do procedures need to be reviewed and updated in response to the rapidly changing technology mentioned by Professor Bork? How should various classes of users be charged (if at all)? How much effort should be mobilized to stay ahead of the moving target of computer technology?

Although the above list is by no means exhaustive, it implies that there is a great deal of scope for an active administrator. However, in fact, the scope for action is severely limited for several reasons. Often in universities we are dealing with over-constrained systems so that the trajectory of action is not subject to much administrative initiative.

Barriers and Forces

Administrators can act through an understanding and manipulation of the forces for or against a course of action. An earlier study carried out by EDUCOM (Anastasio, 1972) provides a useful list of factors inhibiting the use of computers in instruction. Administrators must plan how their organizations will deal with the obstacles that were found to be important:

- Inadequate production and distribution facilities for good quality computer-based instructional materials
- Lack of persuasive demonstrations of computer-based instructional materials
- Lack of an adequate instructional theory
- The established pattern of instruction and role of the teacher
- Cost of computer-based instructional materials

The lack of good computer courseware that can be easily and cheaply acquired is often mentioned as an obstacle. It is also a chicken and egg problem since without widespread instructional computing systems in place, entrepreneurs are not likely to commission much courseware development (Luehrmann, 1977). Without a library of good and readily available courses, colleges are unlikely to invest in hardware. As Professor Bork in his paper and Luehrmann in an earlier paper (1977) have pointed out, the unique characteristics of the videodisc and the microcomputer offer opportunities to solve this problem. The cheap microcomputer may make computing as ubiquitous as the hand calculator. Availability of computing will stimulate authoring talent and promises a market that should interest commercial courseware developers. The videodisc, because it is difficult to copy, may encourage a royalty-based system that filters for talent with relatively small costs to society as a whole. Nevertheless, some social inventions provided by administrators would surely help things along.

It is my hope that the lack of persuasive demonstrations will be remedied shortly. Administrators must find time to pay attention to the demonstrations, to help mobilize the attention of the higher education community, and to follow through on the implications of a compelling demonstration. It will be difficult to get administrators to pay attention to even the most persuasive demonstrations, but it must be done.

The need for theory-based development of computerized instructional materials is beginning to be expressed by an impressive number of observers. One hopes the message will be carried to the administrative offices of private and government funding agencies. Although there is a large amount of knowledge waiting to be synthesized into a theory, it will probably take many years before a useful theory is available to supersede intuition and passion.

The EDUCOM report stated that the established pattern of instruction and the role of the teacher are obstacles. To change them, a new organizational structure is needed. If university structure is changed to fit the technology, people will use the organization and the technology in new ways. The new structure will be best used if some factor prevents reversions to the old structure.

Cost is no longer a valid barrier to adoption and use of computer-based instructional materials, although it is still perceived as an obstacle. Almost any analysis such as the one made by Professor Bork will show that for a small fraction of the total cost of educating an undergraduate student (e.g., $50 per student per year), every student in college can be given significant and educationally important access to an instructional computing system. The administrative problem is to find an acceptable way to plug the costs into the budget and to present the case so that the $50 per student per year is seen as an opportunity by the faculty and other campus powers.

The results, observations, and conclusions of two works (Rockart and Scott-Morton, 1975; Simon, 1976) are particularly relevant and supportive of the argument I wish to make. The forces that will encourage the use of computers are the knowledge explosion, more and better technology, pressures for productivity in education, pressure for institutional cooperation, some student attitudes (student attitudes show as both a positive and negative force), a greater diversity of accepted educational patterns, students' positive attitudes toward technology, the open university movement, the junior colleges' willingness to innovate, and the movement of business into the educational and training field (e.g., the entry of Control Data Corporation into the market). The negative forces are financial stringency, decrease in student enrollment, and faculty attitudes.

Rockart and Scott-Morton observe (p. 232):

> Throughout the seventies there will not be a great deal of cash available to administrators. Without this discretionary money, one of the major tools in the hands of an administration oriented toward improving the teaching process is blunted. In addition, *financial crises—or even semi-crises—tend to hold the attention and over-utilize the time of key administrators, thus diverting their energies* from selling the faculty on the need for improving today's teaching process. [Emphasis added.]

The time and attention of administrators is critical to any remedy, although the effect extends far beyond the time needed to "sell" the faculty.

A point made by many authors has been captured in the following statement by Rockart and Scott-Morton (p. 232):

> Nor would many administrations act decisively to promote technological improvement in the teaching-learning process even were additional funds available. This type of action would violate the traditional (decentralized) university mode of operation.

In a faculty survey conducted in connection with the above work, the faculty themselves rated faculty attitudes as the second most serious obstacle to the use of computers in instruction. Hence, "In most major universities the ability of administrators to vastly influence faculties to change their ways of providing learning assistance is dubious at best" (p. 233).

Simon (1976) makes two points. First, he supports the observation that administrators don't need more information as much as they need something to guide their attention to enable them to process the information. "Attention is the chief bottleneck in organizational activity, and the bottleneck becomes narrower and narrower as we move to the tops of organizations" (p. 294).

Administrators will never know enough, never be able to give the right kind of attention, unless we can educate them to a different world view. Administrators do not yet have the models of an instructional system that will enable them to generalize to the kind of organization needed. I find a visual analogy useful to describe the administrator who tries to devote attention to computer-based instruction in the midst of many other demands on his or her time. In this analogy the administrator is an unfertilized ovum surrounded by hordes of eager sperm trying to penetrate the cell wall. Only one sperm will be selected. By analogy, the administrator's concept of the world will determine what captures his or her attention.

Technology and Organizational Structure

Organizations that succeed with a new technology have created new organizational structures to reflect that technology. Simon (1976) commented on the importance of the organizational structure.

> The division of labor is quite as important in organizing decision making as in organizing production, but what is being divided is different in the two cases. From the information-processing point of view, division of labor means factoring the total system of decisions that need to be made into relatively independent subsystems, each one of which can be designed with only minimal concern for its interactions with the others. The division is necessary because the processors available to organizations, whether humans or computers, *are very limited in their processing capacity in comparison with the magnitude of the decision problems that organizations face.* [Emphasis added.]
>
> . . . When we change the organization we change the picture that the people in it have of the concrete tasks to be done and the concrete goals to be achieved—their concept of the program.
>
> . . . Plans may influence behavior because they provide employees with a conceptual scheme of the agency's program, a scheme that serves as a framework for decisions and action.

The following summarize the situation:

- In the face of restricted funds it is difficult to allocate money to new technologies on campus.
- Faculty are largely resistant to new technology for instruction.
- The organization and tradition of the campus act to neutralize the power of an administrator to effect change.
- If nothing else prevents an administration from being effective, the condition of information overload prevents attention and time from being focused adequately.
- One's model of the organization and the instructional system determines how attention and time are allocated.

To the above list I would add the following: The university's organizational structure enables it to be successful with its present technology—the technology of books and classroom instruction. This same structure, however, inhibits its ability to be successful with a new technology—the technology of computers and electronic communications. To use the new technology, a university structure will have to be created or will have to evolve that will encourage productivity in the new technology.

Since most universities are successful by their own standards, there is little incentive for change. Probably, as with most new technologies, instructional computing wedded to electronic telecommunications will get its start by finding a new clientele that the present system is not serving well. For this reason, Professor Bork's interest in the open university concept is well taken. The new clientele (for the new technology) is ideally one that cannot be adequately served by the old. The technology stands its best chance in a new organization, serving a new clientele, and employing a new structure designed for productivity in the new setting.

The British Open University is probably the best approximation of the ideal situation that has evolved to date. Its departure from the traditional model is instructive. British Open University clientele could not be served by existing British universities. The clients could be served through telecommunications technology. As a result of necessity, BOU organized course teams for the production of outstanding instructional materials and separate teams for the delivery of the courses. However, the faculty is still organized into departments and an academic senate has considerable veto power. Judging from reading and conversations with several of the people involved, this remnant of the present campus system has impeded the ability of the British Open University to continue to adapt to the use of technology for course delivery.

Some Practical Suggestions

If the new college organization is to encourage productivity in the new technology, the following steps need to be taken:

- *Course development and course delivery teams must be basic organizational units.* Funds and rewards for faculty should be based upon productivity and excellence in course development and delivery. My own experience at the University of Mid-America confirms the value and practicality of this approach.
- *Disciplinary and interdisciplinary research should be organized separately from the instructional effort.* Faculty could work in both areas, but the research institutes on campus should not have power over the instructional system.
- *The people in charge of the instructional technology should have a large amount of fiscal and organizational autonomy.* As long as they also have the responsibility to be productive and excellent, they will not misuse fiscal and organizational autonomy. Top administrators cannot know enough or pay enough attention to play a significant role in developing instructional technology.
- *Development and use of instructional technology should be combined with a serious effort to develop more powerful models of learning.* Such models must incorporate knowledge from many disciplines that has implications for educational design.

Technology and Social Networks

The evidence available to me suggests that, for sustained effort, most people benefit from being embedded in a social network. The behavior of many seems to be strongly affected by their perception of the expectations of the people around them. Although the affective power of instructional media (e.g., dramatic force of television) can, to a certain extent, compensate for social isolation (Lipson, 1977), student completion and general persistence are positively affected by personal contact, a sense of belonging to a community, being surrounded by people who know and care. The practical administrative implication is twofold. To build a new system for the employment of educational technology, a social network should be encouraged and designed for administrators who support the use of educational technology, and a similar network should be formed among faculty and others who develop the technology.

References

Anastasio, Ernest J., 1972. "The Study of Factors Inhibiting the Use of Computers in Instruction." A brief report on an EDUCOM research project for the National Science Foundation, EDUCOM.

Bork, Alfred, 1977. "Instructional Systems." EDUCOM Fall Conference, Minneapolis, 27 October.

Lipson, Joseph I., 1977. "Technology and Adult Education: A Report on the University of Mid-America Experiment." *Technological Horizons in Education,* vol. 4, no. 6 (September/October), p. 36.

Luehrmann, Arthur W., 1977. "Intelligent Videodisc Systems—Implications for Education." In *Computers and Communications: Implications for Education,* ed. Robert J. Seidel and Martin Rubin. Academic Press, New York.

Rockart, John Fralick and Scott-Morton, Michael S., 1975. *Computers and the Learning Process in Higher Education.* McGraw-Hill, New York.

Simon, Herbert A., 1976. *Administrative Behavior.* 3rd ed. New York: The Free Press.

14

Instructional Systems: Reaction and Overview

Richard W. McCoy

Introduction

While it is a pleasure and a privilege to respond to the papers of Professors Bork and Lipson, it is also a challenge. A part of that challenge stems from my own absence from direct involvement in instructional systems in the recent past. I am therefore particularly indebted to my colleagues at the University of Wisconsin, Larry Travis and Donald McIsaac, who tried to help me get up to date. They will each recognize their thoughts and suggestions in the paragraphs that follow.

My task is "reaction and overview," but the two papers which have preceded this have done such a good job of overview that I prefer to concentrate on reaction. Before I do so, however, I would like to underscore two points identified in Professor Bork's paper, and would like to add two. I believe the four items are important enough in the context of instructional systems that they deserve special mention here.

Underscores and Additions

The stand-alone, one-on-one computers described by Professor Bork with price tags of $600 have great potential for instructional use. There is a great deal still unknown about just what impact these new and fantastic devices will have on colleges and universities, but it is certain to be dramatic and challenging. I would therefore like to leave a message with those responsible today for large machine computing centers: *Go out and buy one . . . or a few!* They will have little impact on a center's capital budget, and experience with this class of machine is one of the things a center should have in order to prepare for its future.

Two competing technologies described by Professor Bork also have great potential for instruction. The large interconnected systems such as PLATO compete with the small one-on-one systems with videodisc. It is interesting to reflect on the authoring advantages of the first and the marketing advantages of the second; perhaps a kind of symbiotic relationship can be achieved. The opportunity may exist to develop sufficient compatibility between the two to permit the authoring of courseware on the large system with all the advantages of interaction with other authors, test by students, rapid modification, etc. When material reaches a sufficient degree of polish, it could be published on videodiscs for easy distribution.

A third topic that should be singled out and added to the discussion of instructional technology is motivation. The computer has an impressive ability to motivate, to capture the imagination and enthusiasm of a student with such impact that performance on all fronts is increased dramatically. Computer center managers and faculty can recite examples from their experiences of lives changed, of ordinary or perhaps even slow students "turning on" to become top performers as a result of their encounter with the computer.

I'm so impressed with the experiences I've had with this kind of student to believe, to hope, that we can learn to exploit this phenomenon and extend it to at least a few more students. I further hope that many others will be encouraged and interested enough in this special ability of the computer to learn how to put it to work much more generally.

As a representative of the University of Wisconsin, I feel particularly compelled to add some thoughts on the topic of

Computer Managed Instruction (CMI). An early and successful effort was developed in Wisconsin's Economics Department by Professor Allen Kelley, whose "TIPS" program (originally batch CMI, by the way) remains in active use at the UW and elsewhere. This kind of system evaluates performance and permits academic "prescriptions" at the individual student level, the quiz section level, the teaching assistant level, and the level of the entire class. Such systems should be made more generally available and easy to use through both academic and administrative support. They have a great deal to offer to traditional instruction now, where they are easily integrated. In addition, they may provide a valuable base on which to build further capabilities.

A larger CMI effort is currently housed at Wisconsin's Research and Development Center for Cognitive Learning. While this project is directed principally toward secondary education, those involved believe their experience has much relevance to CMI at the university level. I agree with them. Professor Donald McIsaac of this center suggests that "CMI comes first best." If we develop CMI technology now, he believes, we'll receive short-run benefits, but more important, we'll have a critical element needed for future exploitation of teaching/learning systems with more complex dialog. That element involves tracking, evaluation, and reporting of performance at appropriate individual and group levels.

Reaction

In providing a reaction to the previous papers, I will concentrate on what I believe is their most provocative coverage: the technological, pedagogical, and administrative changes that are prerequisites to the dominance of Professor Bork's third kind of instructional system (direct aid to learning). (The first kind of instructional computing relates to learning about computers; the second is use of the computer for problem solving.) This dominance is to develop by 1990 or the year 2000, or perhaps five years sooner—only eight or eighteen years away!

I am no less enthusiastic about the promise of this kind of

instructional system than are the authors of the previous papers; our efforts to achieve this promise should be high. I'd like, however, to defend the pessimists who believe it will take longer. In order to do so, I will outline some of the encouraging factors of the previous papers and will develop in somewhat greater detail the key inhibiting factors which have been pointed out by Professor Bork and Professor Lipson.

The balance between these positive and negative factors may determine the appropriate degree of optimism about early dominance of computers as a direct aid to learning.

Encouraging Factors

Professor Bork's paper has supported the essential encouraging factors for early dominance of computers as a direct aid to learning. They are:

Technological progress. Great strides have been made in the development of authoring systems, inexpensive computing hardware, videodiscs, the advent of the home computer, and more.

Cost effectiveness. The enormous rate of improvement in computing cost effectiveness is being sustained and promises economic feasibility for this application soon.

Estimating error. Tradition has it that in technological areas, developers tend to overestimate short-run accomplishments by a wide margin and underestimate the long range by an equally large amount. The prediction of computer dominance in direct aid to learning by 1985 is a long-range forecast.

Outside pressures. Faculty are experiencing a substantial push from students and are certain to feel it more strongly from them and from other components of the educational process as more and more direct learning aids are used for industrial and commercial training, vocational training, secondary schooling, and continuing education. Home education courseware for purchase by parents is also being added quickly to the marketplace.

These factors and others tend to tilt the balance in the optimistic direction.

Inhibiting Factors

On the other side of the balance are factors that may slow the rate of development or that may tend to support more conservative forecasts:

Technological utopias. Experience in forecasting technological utopias has not been good. Analysts have found it interesting to compare forecasts made in the 1940s for the city of the future with the reality of that future—our present, the 1970s. We were promised monorails, helicopters everywhere, green and open spaces. We got slums, crowding, crime, economic disaster—and a very few helicopters overhead to report the smog level. (Perhaps this is the result of the very significant administrative problems which Professor Lipson has identified?)

Conservative faculty. It will take a generation or more—thirty or forty years is not unlikely—to overcome the inertia of those on some college faculties who lecture from old and yellowed notes and don't know of another way. In their tenure decisions, these professors are creating the next generation of faculty in their own image. While I have no quantitative data, I share with Professor Lipson and others an opinion based on several specific cases which suggests that young, enthusiastic faculty who embrace the computer in lieu of more traditional tools of teaching and scholarship are adding additional obstacles and risks to their quest for tenure.

Human needs. In addition to the conservative, old-school faculty, others will resist the trend. Some of the strongest innovators and practitioners of the third kind of instructional system may also do so in time. One colleague of mine sought enthusiastically to exploit the tools already available in direct aids to learning. His intention: to use the time spared for personal, Socratic interaction with individual students. But they came even less than they had before. In the absence of traditional class contact, the "handshake" did not occur which would bring students to individual sessions. This instructor found out a great deal about his own needs for interaction with students, and is now less certain about the replacement of traditional teaching modes.

Administrative inertia. College and university administrative structures have fully as much inertia as do faculties. Development of computing as a direct aid to learning will require massive reallocations and new resources at a time of declining enrollments. This is a great deal to expect given the difficulty we've had in reallocating college and university resources even in times of more generous budgets.

The medium not the content. Perhaps the most significant inhibitor is the lack of quality content in computer-based instructional materials. It is as if the printing press had just been invented but authors still hadn't written the books. It may not require the four to five centuries necessary to develop the book to its present state, but it will take many decades (some suggest generations) before the great artists of the media appear. Old material presented in the new medium is not art. A generation may pass before teachers appear with the art and style to produce aesthetically interesting learning materials. In the meantime, as long as there are good textbooks available, educators will continue to exploit them.

Educational standards. A special case may exist for graduate education, which is in some measure an apprenticeship system in which students learn not in lectures and exams, but by their own work, reading, and thinking. The role of the faculty here is screening and standard setting of a kind that may not be adaptable to dialog systems, to quantitative measures, or to review of written work. Standard setting is essential to the quality of education and to the need of society. This kind of standard-setting role may be a special challenge to the third kind of computing use and to the open university.

The balance position may now be tipped toward the side that says it will take longer than eight to eighteen years before dominance is achieved by the third kind of instructional system—direct aid to learning.

In the Meantime

Whether or not one shares my distrust of the optimistic forecasts, there will be many years of effort in continuing to build our more basic instructional contributions. Colleges must still find the resources and the administrative response necessary to fully exploit instructional systems for learning about computing and for problem solving. The technology is here, though it can certainly be extended, and the administrative procedures have been demonstrated at Dartmouth, Waterloo, Michigan, and elsewhere. Institutions are nonetheless still failing to support students with adequate access and adequate resources. Providing this support may keep them very busy for the next ten years.

One obstacle is just now being overcome. At Wisconsin, computer center management installed a full charge back system seven or eight years ago which requires each department, each customer, to pay fully in real dollars for work done at the computing center. An unforeseen result has been the difficulty in the mid-1970s of extending the right of computer access to all students. Previously, only some students in engineering, business, and elsewhere had enjoyed the privilege. In most of the schools on the Madison campus, a student could compute only if an instructor had obtained budgeted funds for the purpose. Computing managers were able to achieve the highly desirable and long overdue improvement only through the very difficult route of persuading the several deans, in concert, to support a more general right of access. They were asked to pay for it even while their ongoing and directly course-related computing budgets were strained. This administrative problem delayed implementation of widespread computing access for students at Wisconsin for nearly two years.

With a concerted in-the-meantime effort, faculty and administrators may have some chance of meeting a very real current challenge. The challenge is brought by the student who has already had, at the time of arrival on campus, enough computing to challenge the curriculum and to embarrass some conservative instructors who are solving problems less effectively, and enough expectation of computing access to overreach what many of us are now offering. The challenge is abetted by the new impact of home computers. These pressures will be a significant force in shaping what will happen to higher education in the next, immediate years.

INFORMATION RESOURCES

15

Information Resources: Technical Issues

R. M. Hayes

Introduction

In this paper, I'm going to provide a brief review of history of access to and use of "information resources," together with a more detailed examination of the present state of the technology, its applications, and some projections for the near future.

First, the overview will focus on applications rather than the technology as such. I will not discuss technical details of computers, communications, microforms, or other technological advances. Most college administrators with responsibility are thoroughly familiar with the technical aspects of these technologies. However, I am going to consider the state of usage of these technologies by universities for access to and use of information resources.

Second, even the term "information resources" will be taken, in a fairly limited sense, to encompass only formalized information resources—essentially libraries, data base services, information centers. The overview will not include various kinds of informal information resources like personal files or teleconferencing except as they may be encompassed by the more formal ones.

Review of History and Present Applications

A brief review of the history of the past ten years will set the stage for the present and future of applications of the technology to formalized information resources. Such applications include the mechanization of indexing and abstracting services, the increasing availability of numerical data bases, the development of commercial data base services, the creation of various state and regional library networks to facilitate library cooperation, the distribution of library catalog data, and the implementation of library technical processing systems.

The starting point for this review is a set of projections I made as part of a meeting sponsored by the federal government about twelve years ago. These predictions were subsequently published as part of the *Handbook of Data Processing for Libraries* (New York: John Wiley & Sons, 1974). At that time, I distinguished various activities as either operational (in day-to-day service, on an economic basis, in several university libraries), developmental (more or less in day-to-day service but in only a few libraries and not necessarily on an economic basis), experimental (not at all operational, although technical feasibility is clear), and speculative (in which technical feasibility is in real doubt). At that time, I projected that during the five-year period 1975 to 1980 the following would be operational:

> Nearly all of the clerical activities in libraries should be operational in a combination of on-line and batch modes (on-line for most of the input of circulation, acquisition, and cataloging data; batch for most of the processing and bulk input). Union catalogs for the holdings of various groups of libraries will be computer produced. The use of magnetic tape catalogs and indexes will be an integral part of library operations, including acquisition, cataloging, and reference; for recent material and highly active material, the use will be through on-line consoles. The use of nationally produced magnetic tape catalogs and indexes by the research community of the country will have been an operational service for some time. The transfer of mechanized data bases between libraries will be operational or nearly so. Facsimile transmission between libraries will also be operational over interlibrary communication networks.

Virtually every one of these projections is now a reality, although there is one major difference in detail. The data bases, both for cataloging and for information retrieval, are now generally accessed by the library from central national facilities rather than from the university itself. Thus the transfer of data bases is not really required since the central national services meet the functional need. Only the development of facsimile transmission has failed to meet expectations.

How did we get here in the past twelve years? There have been six major threads of development:

- Mechanization of indexing and abstracting services
- Mechanization of numerical data bases
- Development of commercial data base services
- Distribution of library catalog data
- Creation of networks
- Implementation of technical service systems

Although mechanization of indexing and abstracting services had been an experimental activity for quite some time before, it really came to fruition between 1967 and 1972 as the National Library of Medicine, Chemical Abstracts Services, National Technical Information Service, and literally dozens of other secondary access services implemented systems. The crucial point, as far as university information resources are concerned, was the availability of the resulting data bases for information retrieval.

A parallel though independent development was the increasing availability of numerical data bases like census tapes, Chemical Registry data, and economic data. The 1970 census tapes, in particular, provided an information resource of immeasurable importance, although one that involved significant problems necessitating a cooperative effort among university libraries.

The development that I did not foresee in 1967 was the emergence of viable commercial data base services such as System Development Corporation, Lockheed Information Systems, and Bibliographical Retrieval Services. These services now provide online access to several data bases with emphasis on the reference retrieval data bases produced by the indexing and abstracting services.

The crucial step in distribution of library catalog data was taken in the late 1960s when the Library of Congress began distribution of magnetic tapes to libraries throughout the country. The tapes were called MARC tapes, with the acronym derived from "machine readable cataloging." The establishment of centers to provide online access to library catalog data bases was something I had not anticipated, but it has brought the online catalog to a near reality. OCLC (the Ohio College Library Center) is the largest and most well established computer-based library cataloging service. BALLOTS is a comparable service based at Stanford University. The Washington State library network represents the model of regional centers which I think are likely to be the organizational structure in the future.

The fifth thread, an organizational one rather than a technological one, is the creation of library and information networks. NELINET, SOLINET, CLASS, MIDLENET, and others differ in structural detail, in geographical coverage, and in services provided. However, they constitute organizational frameworks within which the technological threads have been, or will be, woven together.

The implementation of technical services systems has been far less spectacular and visible than the other threads of development, but it has resulted in operational systems for acquisitions processing, for circulation control, for handling of serials records, and so on. Some systems, especially those for circulation control, are commercially available, with well established costs and virtually "turnkey" installation.

The Technical Issues

These several threads, woven together and interacting with each other, provide the fabric of today's mechanized information resources on the university campus. What, then, are the technical issues involved in the implementation and use of the systems available today? I'll review them in four categories:

- the technology,
- the applications,
- the costs in comparison with the benefits, and
- the problems.

There are a few significant aspects of the technology that should be highlighted. (1) Computer output microform is having a major, though unheralded, impact in libraries in colleges and universities. It is being used with increasing frequency throughout the applications I will discuss. (2) The concept of distributed computing, with minicomputers (or, eventually, microcomputers) communicating with central facilities, has not yet had any impact in information resource applications, although there is heavy use of intelligent terminals. (3) The pace at which data bases grow is exceeding that at which the storage technology is improving, and the costs of storage are becoming a major operational burden. (4) The communications revolution has had virtually no effect, although it has been discussed and envisioned as having a radical impact on libraries. Witness the total lack of progress in facsimile transmission, in use of cable television, or in any of the other aspects of advanced communications.

The applications of the technology occur in virtually every aspect of library operations: reference, numerical data bases, cataloging, technical processing. Only document delivery has not yet been significantly affected.

First, in the area of reference work, the services available either on campuses or through commercial services provide access to nearly one hundred different data bases. Some of the fields covered are agriculture, education, chemistry, history, petroleum, oceanography, art, biological sciences, economic statistics, energy, environment, management, medicine, current events, psychology, social sciences, and physics. Services can be used for immediate search of current material or for the full retrospective coverage of a field of interest (at least to the extent included in the data available on line). The significant point about these services is the availability not only of the data bases but of the software for maintenance and search of files. One can therefore visualize, in principle, gradual extension of their services to incorporate maintenance of more specialized, tailored, and personalized files to which the user may add records. The usage of these services has been almost totally by researchers, but there is great potential for their use in support of instruction.

It is important to recognize that the use of these services is not simple, and the vision of each scholar tapping into them from his or her own console, while feasible in principle, is still very much a vision. Each service differs from the others in its protocols and available user commands. These differences reflect the different contexts in which each service was developed. SDC's service is based on its contract work with the National Library of Medicine in development of MEDLINE. Lockheed's is based on its comparable work for NASA, and BRS's is based on a package developed by IBM for its internal dissemination service. Each of the data bases differs also in its subject authority, on which searching must be based, as well as in its format and data structure. The library thus will play a crucial role, in providing both professional assistance needed for access and supporting tools.

Second, in the area of numerical data bases, there has been a much more sporadic development of resources and of services. Some data archives have been created, but only the U.S. census has mounted a major impact on university information services.

Third, in the area of cataloging, the availability of online bibliographic data from OCLC, BALLOTS, or comparable services has permitted libraries of all kinds to provide more accurate and more rapid cataloging of both current acquisitions and backlogs. Most users currently are obtaining the standard 3"-x-5" cards from these services for merging into existing card catalogs. However, two major developments, mutually supportive of each other, are having a major effect on library catalogs. The first is the increasing production of catalogs, or at least of current additions to them, in microform using COM techniques. The most important result is likely to be easy distribution of copies of the catalog of a collection to many points on a campus. The second is the ease of merging the machine records from several campuses into a union catalog—the essential tool for any cooperative program. The potential interaction between these two developments is evident. By distributing union catalogs in microfiche form, either as a supplement to online availability or as replacement for it, access will be made available from many more locations. In any event, the net effect on the catalog as a major information resource on a campus will be profound. Increasingly, we will see the card catalogs of major institutions being closed, with current cataloging (perhaps even retrospective cataloging) being available only in other forms. A second result, already incorporated into some of the existing systems, will be the feasibility of machine retrieval applied to the catalog data base, much as it is applied to the several reference data bases. However, there is one major technical problem that each library using these systems must solve—authority control.

Fourth, in the area of technical processing, the online cataloging services provide some capabilities in support of other functions like acquisitions. However, generally, technical processing systems, including circulation control, seem to be localized to the institution. This means there is much less standardization, a less clear picture of costs or of benefits, and more complications in the development and installation of systems. On the other hand, the potential benefits in these application areas, especially with respect to improved management of a collection, will ultimately be far greater than benefits in the area of cataloging. Mechanization of catalog data was a crucial and essential first step, but later steps will have greater impact.

Fifth, with respect to access to the collection itself or to what is referred to as document delivery, there has been negligible impact of technology. As I've already indicated, the visions of facsimile transmission, of cable television, even of online digital access to the content of books, journals, and reports have been just that—visions. The only major development has been the distribution of government reports and some journals in microform. For the great bulk of material wanted from library collections, access is only through hard copy—either the original or a photocopy.

Further adding to the rather dismal picture with respect to document delivery is the procedure of interlibrary loan by which we still get access to material stored at other libraries. It's expensive: the cost of borrowing totals well over ten dollars per request, divided about equally between the borrowing and lending institutions. It's slow: typical delivery times range over weeks. It's also relatively unreliable, with 30 to 40 percent of the requests unanswered.

It seems clear that some technological breakthrough in this area of application would provide immense payoff. I'll turn to that issue when I discuss projections into the future.

Is it all worthwhile? Are the benefits commensurate with the costs? Is there sufficient return from investment in installing mechanized systems to justify doing so? I'm afraid the answer must be a Scotch verdict—not proven. Let's look at each area in turn.

First, the costs of reference data base use are significant, ranging from ten dollars per contact hour to as much as ten times that. The campus faces a real dilemma in funding the use of these resources. Options include offering the service free to the user and funded by the library; charged to the user; or as some mix of the two, perhaps depending upon type of user.

Counterbalancing costs must be benefits. When free systems (such as the early MEDLINE service and the several campus-based systems) were instituted, there were rapid, nearly exponential increases in the utilization of them. When users were charged even relatively nominal fees the usage dropped off significantly but then began to rise again. Commercial services have charged from their inception, and everything indicates that usage of them is continually rising. This experience suggests that there is indeed an appropriate balance of costs and benefits, at least as exhibited in a market economy. The issue thus comes down to how the campus wants to resolve the dilemma of how to pay for the costs.

Second, the costs of numerical data bases vary so widely and services are so specialized that no generalities can be given. The U.S. census, however, was a special case. In their original form as distributed by the Bureau of the Census, tapes cost well over $100,000. The cooperative program of the Association of Research Libraries resulted in reformatted tapes which could be distributed at about 10 percent of the costs of the source tapes. The benefits from availability of these tapes are clear. The tapes are essential tools in a broad range of research in the social sciences. A major university would be very handicapped without having these data readily accessible on campus.

Third, the costs of use of the cataloging systems are now quite well identified—perhaps $2.50 per title cataloged. However, it is very difficult, in fact, presently impossible, to justify these costs on the basis of compensatory reductions in costs from present manual operations in the large university. Furthermore, there is a real likelihood that the costs of the online services will rise in time, especially if the online files continue to grow. Where then do the compensatory benefits come from? Three facts in particular are significant. The use of these systems is greatly improving cataloging throughput, thus permitting the reduction of backlogs and getting data into the catalog more rapidly. Replacement of the card catalog by other media promises some major benefits. Perhaps most important, the feasibility of providing access to union catalogs greatly improves the potential for sharing of resources.

On balance, with appropriate costs assigned to these compensating benefits (based on alternative means for providing them), the cost-benefit ratio for automated cataloging systems clearly favors use of them. However, each institution should do its own analysis of these assignable costs.

Fourth, the costs of the various technical processing systems cannot be generalized. Each institution will need to do its own cost-benefit analysis here as well. There is just one caveat I would record. The costs of conversion to a mechanized system for technical processing are major capital investments. Whereas the reference data bases or online catalogs represent national investments spread over large numbers of users, the conversion of serial record files, vendor files, in-process files, book identifications, and so on are all costs incurred by the single institution. So also are the costs incurred in conversion of procedures. All of these costs, and the appropriate time period for amortization of them, should be included in a cost-benefit analysis.

Finally, I've already commented on the costs of document delivery. There ought to be a good payoff from a system that provides rapid, economic, and effective access to and delivery of desired material. Librarians still wait for that breakthrough, however.

Some of the problems of information resources, of a technical rather than an administrative nature, have already been implicit in my comments. First, there are costs that are major investments, especially in conversion of files. The national efforts have alleviated some of those costs but by no means all of them. Capital investments in the present means for performing the same functions also deter librarians from investing in computer-based data processing systems.

Second, in the areas of reference data bases, numerical data bases, and bibliographic data bases, there is a fundamental disparity between their sizes and the density of usage. Whereas administrative files are likely to have between 1 and 10 percent of their records active each processing cycle, these information resource files rarely experience as much as .01 percent activity. Thus the costs of online storage can be spread over only relatively small utilization.

Third, many computer-based information resources are still unacceptable to the librarians and faculty who must use them. For example, microforms provide a very cost-effective medium for distribution of information, especially in view of COM techniques, but they have still not been generally accepted. Librarians have been very dubious about the value of automated systems—not simply because librarians are especially conservative or frightened, but rather because the costs are so great and cost-benefit value so marginal.

Fourth, the data involved in these information resource systems are inherently complex, and problems of data reliability are compounded by problems in font and in format. Library rules for cataloging and filing are complex because the data are complex. The result is that the processing systems must deal with problems far different and far more variable than those in administrative data processing, in research computation, or in instructional data processing.

Fifth, there are several legal problems complicating the operation of systems for access to and use of information resources. They are copyright (as it affects any system for document delivery), security and privacy (as they affect data bases with limitations of their availability), and ownership (especially with respect to data bases).

The Future

Most of the dreams envisioned fifteen years or so ago have become operational realities. Mechanized systems for access to and use of information resources in the university exist: they are effective; they are close to being economically justified on the basis of benefits received; there are problems with them, technical, economic, legal, but none seems to be unsurmountable.

Where then do we go from here? I wish my crystal ball were clear enough to see even briefly into the future. Unfortunately, as I've moved into administration, I've lost more and more touch with reality. The basis for projecting into the future is getting pretty out of date, and the crystal ball is cloudy. However, there are some things that I would like to project, as directions of development, if not milestones in the future of development.

Increasing use of microforms. The effect of COM has been to accelerate the pace with which microforms have become integrated into the information resources of the university. They are being increasingly used in internal operations of libraries, as part of the collections of libraries, as means of document delivery.

Within the coming five years colleges will see microforms in a dominant position at least for the internal functions of the library. Within ten years they may be the dominant form of publication and distribution.

Increasing use of distributed computing. Today's systems are either stand-alone (for the technical processing in the library) or they utilize large central facilities, directly online. The impact of distributed computing will be fully as great on the use of information resources as it will be in other parts of the university.

Within the coming five years, a significant number of university libraries will have minicomputers functioning in a shared computing relationship with the large central facilities.

Integration of microforms and distributed computing. When I made my own projections twelve years ago, I had estimated that the use of "microform consoles," connected with and operating under the control of computers, would be in development (as far as university information resources are concerned) during the period 1975 to 1980. I still feel that is the case and that they will be operational within the coming five years. Integration of the computer, acting as the indexing device, the retrieval unit, and the controller, with microforms, in order to access information, is now technically feasible and is operational in some commercial contexts.

Development of document delivery systems. This is an area of such evident payout, with such a variety of technological approaches, that significant experimental work should take place on it during the next five years. However, the problems of costs, of file sizes, of procedures for access are so great that developmental projects and operational systems will probably not be evident within that same five-year period. It will be at least ten years before libraries develop an economical, effective means for mechanized document delivery. Certainly, though, this is a most fruitful area for future development.

Numerical data bases. While the reference and bibliographic data bases seem to be well in hand, with straightforward means for access to them and clear pictures of cost for such access, the future with respect to numerical data bases is relatively chaotic. Few campuses now have established formal procedures for access to them, and there are no centralized services except the U.S. census. Within five years, because of the impetus generated by the 1980 census, we will see national efforts to gain control of numerical data bases as information resources.

Text data bases and text processing. Fifteen to twenty years ago, many researchers had high hopes for solving the problems in mechanized processing of text such as language translation, information retrieval from natural language text, and so on. I had no such expectations and felt, twelve years ago, that significant text processing would still be speculative today and in 1980. I am now torn between wishful thinking and continuing skepticism in this area. However, there are three reasons to believe that within the next five to ten years colleges will see a major research breakthrough in this area. First, there is an immense amount of primary text now being generated in machine-processible form. Thus it is feasible to conduct experiments that would have been impossible even ten years ago. Second, word processing has become so much a part of clerical processing that word processing has become an industry in itself. Programs and procedures for ready manipulation of text are available off the shelf and are economical to use. Third, there is a sense of reality in the present research efforts in text processing, cautiousness generated by being once burned. Solid results, rather than publicity puffs, will be generated. Instead of the false claims that resulted from the pursuit of the federal dollar, there are now real facts of scholarly research. Sometime after 1982 but before 1987 an experimental text processing capability should be available, perhaps affiliated with a development facility for document delivery from an online text system.

16

Information Resources: Administrative Issues

Richard L. Van Horn

To most informed observers, the level of technology available to libraries far exceeds the level of application. Much of the technology appears relevant and, in some cases, of economic merit at the present time. In addition, libraries face both a financial crisis and a role identity crisis, events that should trigger a search for viable alternatives. Thus the glacial slowness with which libraries are embracing new technology certainly deserves attention and explanation. The focus here is on management policy with respect to libraries as information resource centers at colleges and universities.

The Library Environment

Libraries hold a central position in the information storage and dissemination activities at colleges and universities. There are more than 2,500 college and university libraries in the United States with approximately 600,000 holdings and annual operating expenditures in excess of $1 billion. Many of the libraries are of modest size. The Association for Research Libraries with membership restricted to major research libraries by a set of holdings and budget criteria has approximately 80 members. Academic libraries, to some extent at least, are supplemented by about 19,000 public libraries and 8,000 special libraries, many of which are associated with business firms.

Library expenditures represent a significant portion of academic budgets. Library direct operating costs, including salaries and purchase of material but excluding costs of space and other overhead, tend to range from 1.5 to 7 percent of education and general operating expenses (Lave and Miller, 1977). Engineering schools tend toward the lower end and major comprehensive universities with strong liberal arts traditions toward the upper end of the range. Cost per student falls between $100 and $600, cost per faculty member between $1,000 and $8,000, and cost per degree granted from $200 to $2,600. Where per student costs are compared to tuition or per faculty cost to faculty compensation, they clearly are of significance to university administrators.

Libraries increasingly tend to be labor intensive. Collections grow ever larger over time and thus demand more staff time for their maintenance. Wages traditionally have increased and probably in the future will increase faster than inflation. Lave and Miller (1977) found the labor component of direct cost ranging from 50 to 90 percent with a median around 70 percent. In this environment, managers face the following options: (1) library budgets must increase faster than inflation, (2) productivity must increase, (3) the nonlabor component of book, journal, and other material purchase must decrease, or (4) the staff must shrink. In recent years one can observe all of the above in various combinations. Continuing budget increases in excess of inflation for libraries are unlikely, and productivity increases have a limit. Some reductions in staff and material expenditures actually may improve cost-benefit performance as services of low value are eliminated, but at some point reductions must noticeably lower the usefulness of the library.

The prices of library materials have increased faster than inflation for the past several years and probably will continue to do so for the next decade. Average prices of library materials in the United States are believed to have increased over the previous year by percentages shown below (*Bowker Annual*, 1977, pp. 333–335; see also White, 1976).

	1974	1975	1976
Books	15%	15%	8%
Periodicals			
All	9	12	13
Engineering	4	9	20
Chemistry and Physics	16	17	13
Serial Services	6	8	10

Price increases vary by discipline, with science and technology facing the most severe increases. The situation is the proverbial vicious circle. As prices increase, librarians reduce purchases to remain within budgets. Producers face heavy fixed costs; and, as sales volumes go down, prices must go up independently of inflation. The problem is particularly severe because increasing labor costs tend to squeeze the part of the library budget available to materials.

Finally, the information explosion goes on unabated. The number of journals continues to increase. (See King, 1976, for extensive data on the science and technology segment of the information universe.) Emphasis on multidisciplinary, problem-oriented research has generated a large number of new areas in which libraries face pressure to build collections. The new copyright law may result in additional income to publishers (and additional expenses for libraries and users), but it is more likely to simply reduce the level of services available to users as librarians cut back on copying and interlibrary loans. Users who place a high value on an item in most cases will arrange to have regular access to an original. The copyright law will primarily affect marginal users, who may prefer to give up access rather than pay royalties for a copy.

Space and facility costs are also increasing faster than inflation, and libraries use large amounts of prime (clean, heated, air-conditioned, well-lighted, well-maintained, secure) space.

Construction costs have increased more rapidly than inflation, as has the price of land if it is available at all. Energy costs are forecast to rise at rates of 12 to 20 percent annually, and libraries are occupied for many hours each day, often seven days a week. A library that operates on an eight-hour, five-day week poses substantial problems for users, particularly students.

Organizational Considerations

From their origin in the Middle Ages until the past decade, libraries occupied the center of the intellectual information system. Apart from lunch and grievances over parking, the library was the single common point of interest and contact for faculty and students. During the 1950s the Copernicus of the information universe arrived with the rapid flowering of a variety of new information mechanisms. Computers were destined to become the most important; but data communications, television, micrographics, and audio-visual devices also were significant.

Apart from their obvious effects, these new information mechanisms have moved libraries from the center of the information universe into a position as one of the several parts of the information resource system. For example, computer expenses have at a number of universities approached or even exceeded the cost of the library. Since the costs of electronic technologies are declining at a rate of 10 to 30 percent per year while costs of traditional libraries are increasing at 6 to 20 percent per year, the laws of microeconomics are clear. To the extent that electronic technologies can be substituted for traditional media and services, the traditional library of books and journals (with or without micrographics) clearly must find that its role in the information resource system is diminished.

When the library occupied the undisputed central position, it could count on broad faculty support to acquire the necessary resources. Much faculty support remains, but with some noticeable differences. At research universities, the most influential faculty rely on preprints and other informal exchange of documents to circumvent lengthy publication cycles—a process independent of the library. Humanists are fascinated by computerized editing and text processing systems, or a variety of audio-visual materials. For ease of analysis, social scientists prefer computerized data bases from census tapes to stock market transaction records. Many scientists spend full time on computation and discussion or exchange of programs for computation. Students interact with self-paced courses that often are self-contained with no reference to library materials. While everyone agrees that the library is still of critical importance, the willingness to give up scarce resources to the library certainly is diminished.

In this environment, most university administrators, in the last few years of financial austerity and the next several decades of declining student populations, are and will be unwilling and often unable to allow library budgets to increase at a rate faster than inflation. Perhaps more to the point, libraries are being restricted to an approximately constant (or slowly declining) share of the total university budget. Libraries perceive great pressure. Beset on all sides with rising prices and demands, faced with faculty and students with long-established expectations of generous, responsive service, and confronted by administrations that now insist upon constant real dollar budgets and constant space, libraries literally face a problem without a feasible solution.

Future Perspectives

If one accepts the view presented thus far, then the clear conclusion that follows is that libraries must change themselves in significant ways if they wish to continue to hold a central role in the information resource systems. Many librarians agree. Yet, as noted earlier, the rate of change is slow.

One can envision the library of the future to contain a strong core collection of heavily used books and journals tailored to the instructional programs of the university. Growth will be limited as lesser used materials are withdrawn from the collection at about the same rate as new material is added. Much of the information now available in printed form will be stored and transmitted electronically via computer. Retrospective journal holdings will be retained in microform to conserve space. The emphasis in library service will shift from storage of materials in house to access to information with document delivery on demand. To provide these services, the library staff will need access to sophisticated reference materials and services. Computer-assisted bibliographic searching will become a standard reference tool, and data bases will become accessible to students and faculty alike. Material will be available in a variety of formats: microforms, videodiscs, films, audio cassettes, or whatever is most efficient or appropriate to the information being presented.

Few will quarrel with the above scenario as at least one manifestation of a desired state. The question is how to get there. As noted earlier, the rate at which changes or innovations have been introduced in libraries appears slower than one might expect. To understand the administrative problems of introducing change in libraries it may help to examine, in some detail, examples of new technology. What are the characteristics of library functions to which technology has been rapidly adapted contrasted to those in which technology has met slow acceptance or outright opposition? One must generalize with some care, but, in this case, specific examples do appear to provide insight into more general problems.

Example 1: Cataloging

Cataloging offers good prospects for new technology. With minor variations, catalog cards hold essentially the same information at most libraries that own a particular title. The process of generating a catalog card is relatively well-defined and mechanical. Libraries, troubled by the costs and purchase price of getting a new acquisition on the shelf, should be receptive to new approaches.

The Ohio College Library Center (OCLC) system represents

one approach to applying technology to the catalog problem. The center provides catalog information from a computer data bank to more than 600 remote users with terminals. When a participating library acquires a new title, it can query OCLC to receive a display or printout of the catalog information. Users can receive a record on magnetic tape of all items for which they have requested catalog data over a specific period. They can also query the data bank for a number of purposes—for example, to find the participating libraries that hold a specific title. Similar services exist in other parts of the country.

The Ohio College Library Center appears to be a successful example of (1) the use of technology and (2) resource sharing. From a user's standpoint, OCLC has several desirable aspects. The initial investment is small. A participating library need only purchase or lease an inexpensive terminal, CRT or hard copy, and provide several hours of instruction to one or two staff members. Operating costs are modest, amounting at Carnegie-Mellon University to slightly over $10,000 per year; and at CMU, operating costs are more than offset by savings in staff. Finally, the group directly affected by the change consists of several catalogers within the library staff. The library users are unaware of any change and most members of the library staff are unaffected.

OCLC also offers some insight on resource sharing. The OCLC system was developed primarily by an entrepreneur at Ohio State University. Most of the current users did not participate actively in managing or financing the actual design, development, or implementation. They joined the enterprise as customers because it offered a service which they believed to be of value.

Example 2: Bibliographic Search

Libraries serve users only to the extent that the users can (1) identify and (2) obtain materials of current interest. Libraries have long recognized that manual search of card catalogs is tedious and incomplete. Over the years a variety of printed indexes and abstract services has appeared and produced good results. The ideal solution for a researcher (short of a highly capable and sensitive graduate student to do the searching) is the facility to interact with a comprehensive and current bibliographic data base for the area of interest. Providing such service is clearly a job for new technology.

The commercial services offered by Lockheed or by Systems Development Corporation are good examples of operational present-day solutions to bibliographic search. The user enters key words from a terminal and receives selections from the data base that meet the stated criteria. However, acceptance of computer search within universities thus far is modest. The capability exists at many libraries, but use is limited.

As in Example 1, the initial investment in equipment is low—a simple terminal. User groups, training, and operating costs partially interact. With an hour of instruction anyone can use the search facility, and a typical search costs $15 to $30. However, multiple searches often are required to identify the specific set of materials desired by the user. A well trained or experienced searcher can reduce substantially the operating costs to find a set of materials. Since training, especially live training on an actual system, is expensive, a standard approach is to train a cadre within the library to conduct efficient or low-cost searches. However, this approach requires the user to work through an intermediary. Direct access for the user community clearly is technically feasible, but it results in either large training costs or larger than necessary operating costs.

The computer search systems to date have supplemented, not replaced, traditional reference services for at least two reasons. First, the existing computer search systems provide good coverage only in some areas, notably in science and engineering, with little or no coverage in other areas. In short, computer search systems are still under development. Second, full replacement of traditional services requires involvement of the broad user community with associated high costs. As a result, the costs of computer search are extra costs to the library or to users that are not covered by savings in traditional services. This cost structure appears to serve as the major limiting force on acceptance of computer search. Little or no faculty opposition to computer search has materialized, possibly because the use of computer search thus far is largely voluntary. As libraries begin or, in some cases, continue to replace traditional indexes and abstracts with computer search, alternatives will diminish and faculty opposition may increase.

The Lockheed and SDC systems clearly exhibit strong resource-sharing features. No single library reasonably can contemplate building and maintaining a large, comprehensive bibliographic data base. Here again two entrepreneurs—in this case for-profit firms—designed and built services and offered them to customers who were not active participants in managing or financing the development.

Example 3: Micrographics

Library collections forever expand. Since use of most materials is infrequent and space is expensive, a technology that offers a dramatic reduction in the storage volume of materials should expect warm if not overwhelming acceptance. Over the past fifty years, a variety of firms and other groups have concluded that micrographics meet the above criteria and thus are a technology whose time has come. To their certain disappointment and sometimes disaster, university libraries, and particularly university faculties, steadfastly have resisted, generally with success.

Some of the resistance may stem from emotion or tradition (e.g., an unthinking preference for familiar printed pages), but a number of valid problems do exist. The main path of technology points to microfiche, but 16-mm and 35-mm film remain widespread. This multiplicity of forms increases cost of equipment and highlights the possibility of making a mistake by investing in the wrong form. In addition, large amounts of material are not available commercially in any micro form.

Micrographics further require a sizable investment in

hundreds of thousands or millions of dollars to convert retrospectively major parts of collections, and they require additional expenditures for microforms of current publications that are held generally as a supplement to hard copy. Although the investment in microforms plus equipment must be paid now, at a time when libraries already face tight budgets, benefits accrue in the future.

Although some faculty members may question the diversion of funds from print to microforms, the more common complaint relates to personal convenience. When the library converts a holding to microforms, the faculty member must convert his or her usage. For the first time in our three examples, the faculty members or other users see the change and have no alternative. Most users view microforms as less convenient than printed pages; thus, they view the change as an attempt to substitute extra user costs for cost savings in the library. Such substitution is perhaps an appropriate, but certainly a provocative, action.

The problems of micrographics often are compounded by halfway measures or, more elegantly, lack of a systems viewpoint. For an initial experiment with microforms, the typical library acquires a few low-cost (and of dismal quality) readers and printers and places them in an unventilated storeroom along with a jumbled collection of uncataloged viewing materials. No thought at all is given to use of the materials in offices or at home, the traditional location for most faculty study of library materials. After such an introduction, faculty enthusiasm or support for microforms is rare indeed.

Each of the preceding examples contains some broad, general ideas. In the current environment, front-end investment funds are scarce. Innovations that require modest, initial investment, like OCLC, commercial search systems, and so on, should find better acceptance than innovations requiring large investment. Most innovations with modest investment will involve resource-sharing; the actual front-end investment may be large, but it is paid over time by many users.

Resource sharing encompasses the idea of many schools

voluntarily joining together to accomplish a task with better cost-benefit performance than each can achieve individually. The examples show that successful resource sharing need not and often will not involve joint management and financing of an innovation. Multischool management and development of new ideas, while sometimes successful, often bogs down in bickering and conflicting or ambiguous direction over design. The alternative of an entrepreneur who designs a product for multischool use (with perhaps ideas, criticism, and interaction from a group of users) has much to commend it.

The literature on innovation and management of change has long recognized the critical role of users, a lesson perhaps, that deserves re-emphasis here. Cataloging involves only a few specialized users and few user-related problems. Bibliographic search involves, thus far, voluntary users working through intermediaries and again few user problems. Micrographics force the participation of the broad user community and have generated a host of user complaints.

The examples also highlight what is best called the transition problem. Although libraries face a number of long-run problems and pressures, there are reasons to view the next ten years as especially difficult. For about five years, many libraries have reduced services in response to financial pressures. Now they need to explore and implement a host of new information mechanisms and services, most of which do not directly or immediately replace existing services. Faculty members tend to oppose the diversion of already limited library funds to support new services, particularly if such supports result in a reduction of traditional services. Thus libraries encounter great difficulties in finding funds for innovation. As a result, most transition to new mechanisms is piecemeal, often unsatisfactory, and in the long run more costly.

Conclusion

Simple solutions to the administrative problems of introducing new services and mechanisms in libraries, however welcome, are unlikely. A first step is for university administrative officers to realize that the library faces some difficult problems, especially during the transition phase, and that solution of these problems requires management attention, support, and resources beyond those normally allocated to the library. While there is much to be said for muddling through, it probably will not work to anyone's satisfaction in this case.

A second step is to reconsider the library in the context of an Information Resources Center. Such a center might consist of the traditional library, the computation center, academic computing, administrative data processing, text processing, publications and printing services, audio-visual services, and instructional television. These activities possess some common technology and most of all a common focus on providing information-related services to faculty, students, and administration. The lines between these areas often result from arbitrary past decisions and indeed vary from school to school with little rationale. The cleanest approach calls for planning for and managing these activities within a single organization unit. Such a unit has existed and operated well for the past several years at CMU. If a single unit is unfeasible, then good coordination and joint planning of facilities and services for all information resource areas may represent a reasonable, although probably less effective, foundation for encouraging innovation.

Most libraries will not and probably cannot support more than a minimal level of innovation out of current operating budgets. Current budgets should go largely to traditional services which are and for a number of years will remain the vital center of the library. During the transition period, innovation will require substantial funds from foundations, private sources, and government or internal reserves. It is important to note strongly that these funds should not go to support research; they should go to exploration, demonstration, and implementation of well-developed and effective new information mechanisms or services. A number of such services are available, often from commercial vendors, and many involve resource-sharing.

In many cases, libraries can profit from better systems planning. Because the structure, services, and technologies of libraries have remained relatively constant for a long time, libraries tend to have limited experience with redesign of these areas. The management of change generally is difficult, but the libraries' lack of experience can compound the problems. However, libraries can hire people with the appropriate skills—for example, recent graduates of some library schools, or management or systems programs. Alternatively, many libraries can find people already on campus with the requisite skills, especially libraries that operate in the context of an information resource center.

Finally, it may be of value to recall once again the well-known fact that colleges and universities, in common with most organizations, have a political side. Despite jokes or complaints to the contrary, administrators in most colleges and universities do not make resource allocation decisions totally on the basis of abstract principles, science, equity, or cost-benefit analysis. The decision process also responds to the preferences, expressed or implicit, of deans, academic department heads, faculty, and students. Libraries can benefit greatly from careful thought and planning on how to maintain a vital role in the information resource system and thereby assure themselves of the continuing support of their constituency.

References

The Bowker Annual of Library and Trade Book Information (New York: R. R. Bowker Company, 1977).

Lave, Judith R. and Miller, David W., 1977. *Library Resources at CMU and Other Universities: A Comparative Investigation.* Carnegie-Mellon University Working Paper, September.

King, D. W. (principal investigator), 1976. *Statistical Indicators of Scientific and Technical Communication,* vol. 2. A National Science Foundation Research Report, King Research, Inc.

White, Herbert S., 1976. "Publishers, Libraries, and Costs of Journal Subscriptions in Times of Funding Retrenchment." *The Library Quarterly,* vol. 46 (October), p. 4.

17

Information Resources: Reaction and Overview

Lee G. Burchinal

Perspectives

My comments represent an attempt to integrate and extend the remarks of Dr. Hayes and Dr. Van Horn. Most observers, I believe, will agree with Dr. Hayes' view that most projections made ten years ago regarding information processing advances have been achieved. Lack of widespread use of facsimile transmission is the major shortfall. Recent developments in data compression combined with digital networks will certainly change this picture in the coming decade.

However, even our most significant achievements, like online searching of bibliographic data bases and shared library cataloging, are still in primitive first stages of development. We have simply applied computer and telecommunications technology to previous manual tasks. In the bibliographic field, computer processing was first applied by abstracting and indexing services to attain more timely printing of their conventional searching tools. In time, the computer tapes became an end product. Today, the online bibliographic searching industry is

---

*Dr. Burchinal is Director, Division of Science Information, National Science Foundation. The views expressed in his paper are exclusively those of the author and are not necessarily the views of the National Science Foundation. This paper is exempt from copyright and is in the public domain.

booming. There are more than 400 bibliographic (and some numerical) data bases containing about 55 million records. About 75 percent of these are accessible on line. In about four years, the number of annual online searches has increased from about 700,000 to 1.5 million. These are notable accomplishments, and reflect two fundamental and significant changes in management and use of information obtained through libraries and information centers. One change involves the substitution of nonprint forms of distribution for the paper-dominated system. The second is the shift from near total reliance on local holdings to extensive use of outside services for accessing large, remote sources of needed information.

These changes in management of libraries and information centers are a microcosm of what is happening in the United States economy. In fact, the driving forces for changes in library and interuniversity communication come from dynamics within the U.S. economy, especially the growing information sector.

Within the next decade, I think, we can confidently expect to see present data base generation, online searching, and document delivery activities mature into integrated, network-based information services. Such development will result in substantial changes in the structure of libraries and information services, revenue bases for operations, and competencies required of library and information professionals and users. Before this happens, however, some difficult obstacles will have to be overcome.

Obstacles

There are at least four sets of obstacles to significant expansion of network-based information transfer services:

- added costs,
- user resistance,
- institutional problems, and
- fragmented enterprise.

General computer-based information services are far more cost-effective than manual searches. Fifteen minutes at a terminal is usually sufficient to produce a thorough search of literature of a given topic. The equivalent time for a comparable search by a trained reference librarian ranges from a day to a week. Clearly, online searching is more cost-effective. However, in terms of most present library budgets, it imposes an *added* expense on top of existing personnel and materials budgets. There are capital costs to acquire terminals and operating costs to meet the hourly charges.

Most libraries, unfortunately, have difficulty absorbing such added costs because their budgets are tight. However, as evidenced by the growing use of online services, some find the additional funds. While charging for services is repugnant to some librarians, others charge for online services in order to provide more effective services to those who can or are willing to pay for them. In this way, part of the cost of online services can be passed on to users.

Users have a number of problems with current library systems for good reasons. Virtually all of today's systems are designed for use by computer specialists or those willing to take considerable time to become reasonably expert in use of a terminal and knowledgeable about the idiosyncrasies of various data bases. Data bases differ in format, content, indexing schemes, protocols, and so on. Casual users simply cannot acquire and retain the skill necessary to access the current array of diverse data bases. As a result, most searching is done by intermediaries, primarily by trained reference librarians or information specialists. Use of additional personnel as intermediaries drives up the costs of searches. This can have the added effect of dislocating library staff and budgeting, which means other services may suffer or the library may have to reduce purchases of books, serials, or other materials in order to render online information retrieval services.

The obstacle of added costs could be partially overcome by

making online services easier to use and by familiarizing users with them. The Division of Science Information of the National Science Foundation was pursuing both approaches in 1977, with about one dozen projects in each area.

Institutional problems present one of the more durable obstacles. Some institutional problems arise from the fact that several different administrative entities in a university have responsibility for information transfer functions that could be far more effectively integrated. Computer centers and libraries, for example, are usually separate entities. Audio-visual centers, records management, and printing and reproduction operations are also often autonomous activities. Yet all of these activities represent different facets of a common process: the capture, distribution, storage, and retrieval of information. Some universities (including Carnegie-Mellon, noted by Dr. Van Horn) have combined library and computer services. Others have integrated audio-visual or learning resource centers and libraries. Some industrial firms have combined a broad range of communication functions including computer services, libraries, records management, and telecommunication services. As information services become a larger portion of college and university operations, integration among now separate communication and information processing activities can be expected to accelerate. University management will, no doubt, be influenced as well.

Perhaps the most serious obstacle to achieving fuller benefits from the potentials of networking technologies is the fragmented nature of the information marketplace. Thousands of publishers supply serials, books, and other materials to thousands of libraries. Print remains the dominant medium, although microforms are gaining broader acceptance. Aside from bibliographic records, very little information is provided in electronic form. Changes that would allow libraries to operate more effectively have to originate with publishers. The present system of distributing and storing hard copy of materials is no longer cost-effective. Colleges and universities can no longer afford the buildings necessary to house vast paper collections. More cost-effective alternatives exist. As Dr. Hayes indicated, microforms, particularly computer-produced microform (COM), represent one alternative for storage of large volumes of text. Combined with distributive computing, micrographic storage offers a relatively low-cost way to store and retrieve a large volume of material.

However, for libraries and their users to benefit from these technologies, publishers will have to release materials in micrographic, videodisc, or other forms. Therein lies the problem. Changes of this magnitude involve high risks for publishers. Is there an adequate market? Will enough libraries subscribe? What are the economics of these new ways of packaging and distributing information?

Change in this area will no doubt come slowly. Although paper will continue to predominate, microform usage will grow. Fully electronic transmission of information and text will start as an option, just as microforms are today, and will likely grow as well. In time, cost, convenience, and preferences of libraries and users will structure the market for alternative forms of information products and services.

Trends

Despite these real obstacles, information transfer among college and university libraries can be expected to evolve toward network-based access and delivery services. This trend is caused by the driving forces behind the evolution of the U.S. information economy. Information systems and services used by academic libraries will provide the following:

Easier access to diverse data bases through standardization, use of front-end simplifiers, and various user aids such as data base locaters and data base mapping techniques. Research sponsored by the National Science Foundation, through the Division of Science Information, is contributing to these developments.

Further integration of data base searching and document delivery. Today, users can search a data base online and then, for a number of data bases, order documents online. Although delivery is still by mail, delivery time is cut in half. Further advances in facsimile transmission will allow even more rapid document delivery. New products from communication firms are now available; further improvements can be expected.

Coalescence of communication technologies. Paper, micrographic, and electronic technologies are being brought together in more powerful applications of communication engineering. Information may be held in different forms at different stages in the transmission cycle, depending upon systems and use parameters. Material may initially exist in machine-readable form, be converted to COM microfiche for storage, and then be provided to users as hard copy. Other combinations are possible. These trends, as documented by the recent supplement to *Fortune* magazine, "Information Processing and the Office of Tomorrow," are being abetted by requirements to cope with an ever-rising volume of information in a more cost-effective manner. All large organizations—industrial, commercial, academic, and governmental—are faced with these requirements.

By considering information and communication issues, EDUCOM can help universities more fully benefit from these developments.

18

The Technology Transfer Process in Colleges and Universities

Donald K. Smith

Introduction

One of the irreducible problems in the speed of technology transfer in colleges and universities is the roadblock of academic administrators. As a group we seek to assume leadership by judging the direction in which the faculty is moving and then rushing to place ourselves in the forefront—a not inconsiderable skill since the faculty is usually moving in all directions. We also achieve capacity to influence the direction of higher education at about the same rate as we acquire intellectual obsolescence. Thus by the time we are able to change things, we can't think of anything that needs changing.

So, in the spirit of offering a glimpse of your problem in action, I discuss here certain perspectives on the future of computing in colleges and universities, particularly as this future may be affected by distributed computing.

Perhaps a way to start is to tell a story I heard recently in Washington which describes my view of the current situation in higher education if not the future. The congregation of a small and somewhat isolated church had met to discuss the purchase of a new chandelier for the chapel. Discussion was heated and grew increasingly lengthy and acrimonious. Finally an elderly deacon in the rear arose to say, "Why in the name of the Lord are we sitting here talking about using our money to buy a chandelier. Even if we got one, there ain't no one in the congregation who would know how to play it, and besides what we really need in this church is more light."

By stretching a bit, the story may provide entry to a statement of the persistent damper on the speed with which new technology can become integral to, and supportive of, the purposes and uses of human institutions. The essence of the problem is this: new technology must be provided insofar as possible in a form which supports and extends the structures and activities that the users believe essential to their own condition and the nature of their institutions. It must also encounter users whose understanding of the potential of the technology has at least reached the level needed to quicken imaginative receptivity and activity. It must further compete for eternally scarce resources. Therefrom flow many frustrations.

Dimensions of the Problem

Two dimensions of the condition and structure of universities are likely to slow change in the decade just ahead, no matter how logical, cost-effective, or theoretically attractive the direction of change may be.

The first dimension is the climate of fiscal austerity in which we now live and are likely to live for the foreseeable future. It is the most popular topic at gatherings of academic administrators these days, where all discussions begin with the question, "Did you hear what happened to our budget this year?" Administrators are all painfully aware of the fact that national confidence in the "saving power" of higher education has declined substantially in the last decade. A nation oversold on the power of knowledge to lead humankind to early Utopia needed to become more realistic. Since administrators in higher education had some responsibility for the oversell, the task of reconstructing confidence will take time. Moreover, this work, even if successful, does not promise to result in vastly expanded public investment in higher education. Competition for public dollars is at an all-time high, with the claims of welfare, environmental protection, health care, defense, social security, to name only a few, competing within governmental budgets struggling with uncertain growth prospects, unemployment, and inflation. In this context colleges and universities face a long-term struggle for effective survival without many prospects of finding new front-end money to speed up the processes of internal change. In a variant on a current aphorism, "If you can see light at the end of the tunnel, you are facing the wrong direction." The current fiscal climate is an unfortunate but real constraint on the responsiveness of university administrators to even the most persuasive claims for the merit of certain new forms of investment.

The second dimension that slows change has a longer history and is, on balance, to be viewed as a necessary and desirable concomitant of a faculty governance system in universities. Frustrations that administrators encounter in seeking to elicit changes in the habits of professors flow from conditions essential to the nature of universities. To put it even more bluntly, the conservatism with which the professoriat responds to pressure for the incorporation of new technologies into the way in which it does business should be understood as a condition flowing from the nature of universities rather than a perverse human condition needing radical alteration.

Universities are very old institutions whose habits have not been developed casually. To the contrary, universities, at least as they exist today, have developed in western civilization on the basis of about 800 years of experience, spanning the long reach from Bologne, Salerno, Paris, and Oxford in the thirteenth century to the luxuriant variety of present institutions. One can summarize their role in society by relating that role to the concept of knowledge. Universities are, in abbreviated form, institutions charged with recovering, organizing, augmenting, and disseminating the knowledge available to society in any given period of history. They are responsible for assuring the sufficiency and the validity of that knowledge base. This is a not inconsiderable responsibility.

If one assumes that some entity called knowledge exists and that it is usefully known (an assumption not all scholars would grant), responsibility for its condition generates certain organizational imperatives, most of which can be recognized in any respected university. For example, responsibility for knowledge generates the notion of a community or communities of professional scholars—men and women who by aptitude, education, and commitment to truth are willing to devote themselves collegially to tasks of recovery, discovery, and dissemination of knowledge. They must enter an arena of criticism in which both their allegations of facts and their theories are to be subjected to criticism, and the cyclical probabilities of ridicule, revision, or transformation. They must enjoy substantial intellectual autonomy in their work.

The primacy of collegial decision making on matters of instruction, research, and the appropriate behavior of those adjuncts called administrators is not, then, a matter of historical accident. Rather, it is a matter of historical necessity if universities are properly to perform their mission in society. This form of decision making is inherently slow in the aggregate, although occasionally spectacular in generating breakthroughs in knowledge. It views externally generated pressures for a change in habits with suspicion. Further, such conservatism is essential to the importance and difficulty of the central mission of universities. On many days, most faculty may believe that it would be possible to carry out scholarly work if only the students and administrators would go away. Most administrators believe that it would be possible to run an efficient university if the faculty, students, and government would go away; and most students believe that it would be possible to get useful service out of all three if they would only take advice. However, on any day, and in any context of reflection, all three groups must all realize that they are joined in an enterprise which brings all of them into a continuing maze of distributed interactions, free from the burdens of power or the feasibility of productive coercion, condemned to watch good ideas await their time and place, but persuaded that these conditions fit the territory, fit the mission, and have an integrity not otherwise achievable.

One of my colleagues describes the faculty as a self-governing body which can agree that the dean must be hanged, but can't agree on the time and place. There has to be wisdom in a governance structure which permits great thoughts but constrains impetuous actions.

I am postulating that, in good universities, expanded use of technology in common with other good ideas has to battle its way slowly through a decision-making process that is essentially distributed, and essentially conservative. This is an excellent way of assuring the integrity of ideas that survive and the productivity of institutions with responsibility for the integrity of its pursuits.

Distributed Computing for Administration

You can judge from all this that I am not much of an enthusiast for the Fourth Revolution prediction that computing will revolutionize the 800-year-old habit system of university communities by the end of this century. The habit system is not all that irrelevant to the purposes of universities, nor has it been all that unproductive. However, I do not want to leave this discussion on such an unpromising note.

I have thus far referred twice to the university as a distributed universe with distributed centers of decision making and distributed sources of authority—a human community of distributed communities. The uses of the term suggest a possible affinity between the emerging technological possibilities of distributed computing and the characteristic structure of the university. It is this possible affinity that I want to explore briefly in pursuit of a hypothesis that emerging technology may in fact be creating a potential which will speed greatly the processes of amiable transfer and assimilation into the university setting.

These processes have not been so terribly slow. I am constantly struck by the fact that universities have less than thirty years of experience in computing. Administrative computing got its start in the accounting, payroll, and registrar's offices during the 1950s. Both massive incorporation of computing into the research enterprise and tentative feelers into the instructional area became popular after sputnik. Many professors started teaching when the possibilities of computing were no more than a gleam in the eye of a few scientists and a Buck Rogers fantasy for the rest of the university staff. Today a university of any size cannot be run without a substantial administrative computing center equipped with a staff of analysts, programmers, and operators able to make the computers work.

However, the topic before us is "Future Prospect," and this can be best pursued by discussion of both administrative and instructional computing in the context of distributed computing technology.

This discussion gives particular attention to administrative computing and instructional computing. Extensive discussion of computers in research is omitted because this area of university activity is conspicuously free of any issues about necessity, compatibility with the university enterprise, or rate of assimilation into that enterprise. Research has undoubtedly provided the oldest and strongest of the driving forces leading to the current availability in universities of an array of both the larger, faster computers and smaller, special-purpose computers. In a real sense, research needs produced an immediate interface between the possibilities of new technology, and the interests and pursuits of scholars. It produced a drive for bigger and faster computers leading to centralized computing centers, and elaborate mechanisms for allocating use among many candidates. It produced simultaneously a drive from individual scholars or small groups of scholars for distributed computing involving an ever-expanding array of smaller, less expensive special-purpose computers. These simultaneous processes of centralization and diffusion will probably not change much during the next several years. However, the power and size of central computers available within a single university may have peaked, and increased diffusion of smaller, special-purpose research computers may be just beginning. The speed of diffusion of computing in universities will not be governed by resistance from users or doubts about the efficacy of use, but by the familiar constraints of research budgets in the context of general funding constraints for higher education. We may also see increasing emphasis on consortial or interinstitutional uses of relatively expensive special-purpose computers associated with particular lines of research or particular categories of data processing. Another increasing form of constraint will be the current concern of administrators with the longer-term cost consequences of acquiring new special-purpose equipment. It is one thing to say that extramural funding has made lease or purchase of the equipment possible. It is another thing to ask about the consequences of acquisition on austere budgets for physical space modification, energy consumption, and maintenance and replacement budgets. Times have grown so tough in Wisconsin that the University of Wisconsin–Madison recently met the mind-boggling question from state government as to whether or not a gift of two million dollars to construct a badly needed new building should be accepted since construction of the building carried with it enormous continuing costs for heat, light, cooling, and maintenance. In this context, universities will be looking long and hard at equipment acquisition possibilities which would have been immediately cleared a decade ago.

Now let us turn to the area of administrative computing where the possibilities inherent in distributed computing may have important potential for some rather significant changes in direction. To develop this point, I wish to further narrow my focus to consideration of computing as an aid to management decision making rather than discussing the full range of administrative data processing.

In the University of Wisconsin system an Office of Analysis Services and Information Systems supports the work of budget planning and academic planning, and also provides a host of special reports and analyses required to feed the ever-growing appetite of government for more and better information. Student data, financial data, curricular data, and facilities data are all maintained in a centralized computing facility. The maintenance of these central information files in a system involving thirteen universities, fourteen two-year centers, and statewide extension obviously requires a carefully designed data base and the development of a distributed system of information inputs of a nature somewhat different from those which might be envisioned in the more popular conceptions involving minicomputers and microcomputers. However, data elements and data input requirements are now standardized for the system; institution-specific elements of the central files are also generally stored in computing centers maintained by all of the institutions, and a reasonable level of peace prevails across the land—at least temporarily. Getting all of this accomplished was no mean task.

The central data base and system data files are serving processes of management decision making effectively. They are serving requirements for external reporting effectively. Maintenance of them requires ongoing tasks of great importance relating to continuing efforts to ensure the integrity of the data, to develop the technical competence in each of the institutions to provide this assurance, to encourage software exchange, and to lay the groundwork for what might be a promising networking of computer centers. However, the very creation of this massive data capability, together with its potential for continuing expansion, has also brought to light the severity of some not unanticipated problems. One of the problems with data is the eternal potential it provides for inaccurate and inappropriate use. The existence of systemwide data files has an attraction for external and internal analysts who are drawn to discover what new and original hypotheses about the management of higher education might be derived from data. The hypotheses thus derived would immediately carry the plausibility of being grounded in fact—in computerized fact, which is the ultimate sanction.

The potential severity of the problem created by inaccurate and inappropriate use of data was demonstrated two or three years ago in Wisconsin. An enthusiastic analyst from state government, looking assiduously for ways to trim budgets, discovered that the university had a data run on the enrollments in the several thousand courses offered by the several universities of the system. Pencil in hand, he quickly revealed that if the university would only close all courses enrolling fewer than five students, we could dispense with the services of *x* number of faculty, whose salaries, based on systemwide averages, would total *x* millions of dollars. Moreover, the effect on average class size from the removal of several hundred faculty and all small courses would be slight on a systemwide basis, and therefore would be scarcely noticed. This kind of analysis may seem so patently absurd as to be scarcely worth mentioning. However, it involved many university administrators in a long, voices-raised hearing with a legislative committee, replete with solemn and searching questions, and with a kind of uneasy dropping of the matter joined to an implication that the whole approach was probably worth pursuing at some future date. The legislature in its wisdom decided the analysis was faulty, but cut the university budget anyway.

The problem with data is that it seems to shed light, even though it may give little insight into processes fundamental to scholarship. It invites search by persons ill equipped to know what they are seeking or incapable of filling in the fine print that converts data to information and stipulates its limitations.

In the context of universities, there are a number of nontrivial questions which relate to the construction of massive centralized information systems. They include the questions "Who has need to know what?" and "Who has access to what?" If universities could begin developing information data bases hierarchically, with distributed controls and access protocols governing higher levels of aggregation and use, they might remove one of the major political questions harrassing the development of management information systems and the uses of computers in the service of more informed decision making.

In such a construct, fully realized, the need for a system administration to maintain large-scale capability to store and process data would be reduced, and its staff services would be focused more on providing technical expertise on matters of equipment acquisition, systems analysis and design, and maintenance, as well as on analytical studies designed to provide specifically needed information in forms most suitable for decision making.

The road from where we are now to such a future university structure will not be quickly traveled. Problems such as equipment compatibility, software sharing, and policy development are massive. Questions of cost-effectiveness will be of utmost importance. Designing a system of information retrieval much more costly to provide and maintain than that presently at hand would not be greatly rewarding in the presence of austere budgets. I am certain that centralized administrative computing centers are not about to disappear abruptly, nor are they any more likely to fade away wholly than would central libraries in a large university moving toward departmental and collegiate-based libraries or learning centers. However, for highly decentralized and distributed institutions such as universities, the questions of who has access to what, for what purpose, and on what basis of need are both currently formidable, and a persistent barrier to advancement in the uses of computing for decision making. Distributed computing might be the key that unlocks the door to more and better uses of computing for administrative purposes.

Distributed Computing for Instruction

There is an obvious fit between the nature of university organization, instruction, and distributed computing. Without any consideration of computing, it is appropriate to note that instruction is the most widely distributed activity that occurs in universities. For the most part, professors administer a manual system and design their own software. More and more frequently they augment designs for instruction with available audio-visual resources, and there has been a slow but steady increment of enthusiasm for professors, teams of professors, or students working with their professors to develop auto-tutorial packages providing supplementary or alternate ways of accessing learning. All of this takes place, however, within a distributed system of faculty governance over the structure and content of the curriculum. In this context, individual professors, teams of professors, or students working at the direction of professors are now designing and developing their own systems for instructional computing. Professional communication among colleagues in like disciplines and professions, joined to the increasing availability of low-cost hardware, is beginning to encourage wider distribution of instructional software and hardware. If the advancement of instructional computing seems to move slowly, this is not occasion for major new initiatives by university administrators. There are many ways in which faculty who are interested and able can be helped with their own purposes. Technical advisory services can be provided to reinforce self-generated interest or enthusiasm. Within the limits of constant competition for funding, special funding can be sought, or incentive grants provided, for software development. These processes are working. They will continue to work, and they will be facilitated by the availability of more power in smaller computers. Above all, administrators and faculty must stop calling for a revolution in the structure of decision making and change processes in universities in order to speed a potential revolution in the uses of computing technology for instruction. More professors in the future will be publishing software packages rather than publishing textbooks, and that is as it should be.

I have little passion for undue efforts to speed diffusion of technology. I believe our civilization has been well served by distributed centers of authority responsible for such crucial questions as "Among the universes of knowledge available, what formulations of these universes are most valid?" and "Of the knowledge available, what knowledge is of the most worth?" These questions are, and should be, eternally controverted. University administrators will be well advised to emphasize the institutional structures that will keep such questions eternally controverted rather than promote cost-effective distribution of some particular construct.

One of the ways in which universities speed assimilation of new technology is by increasing the number of people who have some understanding of the potential of that technology. There is a considerable movement in colleges and universities to introduce at least introductory study of computing technology into a variety of undergraduate and graduate curricula. Some proponents argue that given the role of the computer in contemporary civilization, introductory knowledge of this technology should be a part of the armament of every citizen seeking higher education or completing any of our degrees. This position has been implemented by some liberal arts colleges. Assuredly the introduction of computing technology is a matter involving change between generations. If the professors of the future, regardless of discipline or professional area, find the computer less of a mystery or threat than may be the case with many of the current crop, then diffusion of its use follows inevitably.

Conclusion

Universities now face not a revolutionary, but an evolutionary, environment in computing—an environment which, through processes integral to the university mission and under press of great resource constraints and great competition for resources, will slow but not check the changes potential in a powerful technology.

Institutions need not go to any great lengths to organize for such change. In administrative computing, the probable decentralization of computing, with computing capabilities coming in smaller and less conspicuous packages, poses at once a threat and a promise. The threat is loss of control over information needed to manage the increasingly complex environment of universities. The promise is better control over the dangers of improprieties in access to and uses of data. To the extent that improprieties can be controlled, decentralized decision making centers will be increasingly free to use computer data. Administrators will need to respect the advice of instruction and research faculty as well as current and potential administrative users as they give their perceptions of the systems which will best fit their needs. University administrators need to hold before them the requirement that development be predictably cost-effective in an environment where resources cannot be readily diverted from the tasks of supporting current instruction, acquiring new knowledge, and supporting our ever-growing commitment to public service. They need to keep in mind that they require integrity and quality in any information gained or transmitted through any computing system.

An orderly transition is predictable from centralized control over computing resources to a more distributed control. This transition may, in fact, fit most fortuitously with the optimal model of university organization and governance.

For Product Safety Concerns and Information please contact our EU
representative GPSR@taylorandfrancis.com
Taylor & Francis Verlag GmbH, Kaufingerstraße 24, 80331 München, Germany

www.ingramcontent.com/pod-product-compliance
Ingram Content Group UK Ltd.
Pitfield, Milton Keynes, MK11 3LW, UK
UKHW022118190926
475702UK00013B/1515
* 9 7 8 0 3 6 7 1 6 7 4 4 8 *